JOHN R. RICE

MOODY PRESS
CHICAGO

Moody Press Edition, 1976

ISBN: 0-8024-9434-X

8 9 10 11 12 Printing/LC/Year 87 86 85 84

Printed in the United States of America

CONTENTS

PREFACE

MANY A YOUNG CHRISTIAN, in the joy of his first love for Christ, is shocked at the idea that he could ever sin. I remember how, in naive and simple love, once I told the dear Lord that I would never, never sin again! But alas, Christians do sin.

On the other hand, some Christians feel that since we have the carnal nature it is inevitable that a Christian must live a poor, sorry life, always a slave to sin, waiting till he gets to heaven for victory and the overcoming life. That, too, is a tragic mistake. Despite the weakness of our flesh, Christians may live in daily victory, daily fellowship with God.

No one should ever be complacent about sin. Sin is the blackest, most terrible and terrifying thing that ever occurred in this world! Sin breaks the heart of God and, if unlamented, unjudged, unrepented of, unforsaken, or unforgiven, brings certain judgment and punishment of God. Christians need to face the sin question. Will you study with me what the Bible teaches about when a Christian sins?

1

ALL CHRISTIANS DO SIN

But if we walk in the light, as he is in the light, we have fellowship one with another, and the blood of Jesus Christ his Son cleanseth us from all sin. If we say that we have no sin, we deceive ourselves, and the truth is not in us. If we confess our sins, he is faithful and just to forgive us our sins, and to cleanse us from all unrighteousness. My little children, these things write I unto you, that ye sin not. And if any man sin, we have an advocate with the Father, Jesus Christ the righteous: And he is the propitiation for our sins: and not for ours only, but also for the sins of the whole world (1 Jn 1:7-9; 2:1-2).

For this cause many are weak and sickly among you, and many sleep. For if we would judge ourselves, we should not be judged. But when we are judged, we are chastened of the Lord, that we should not be condemned with the world (1 Co 11:30-32).

THERE ARE SOME who say that no genuinely converted, born-again Christian sins. They some way think that to be a Christian means one has simply gotten so good that he does not do wrong. But such people, however well intentioned, do not know human nature and do not know the Bible. Christians do sin. All Christians sin. And no Christian can have day-by-day victory over sin and live the happy, joyful, triumphant life until he faces the true facts about sin in his own nature, sin in his own life, what sin will do, and what to do about it.

MANY SCRIPTURES PLAINLY STATE THAT ALL, INCLUDING CHRISTIANS, SIN

Let every doubter, every skeptic, on this question, read some of the plain statements of the Bible.

The beloved apostle John by divine inspiration writes, "If we say that we have no sin, we deceive ourselves, and the truth is not in us" (1 Jn 1:8).

"We" here means the apostle John and the Christians who read the Bible. "If we [Christians] say that we have no sin, we [Christians] deceive ourselves and the truth is not in us." If John, the beloved disciple, should say that he, at the time he was writing this epistle under divine inspiration, had no sin, then he would be self-deceived and would be missing the truth!

Be sure to note that the present tense is used. If I should say at this very moment that there is no sin in me, that I have no sin, I would be deceiving myself. It may be that I am conscious of no sin except what has been confessed and forsaken before

8

God. But remember, the Scripture teaches, that "The heart is deceitful above all things, and desperately wicked: who can know it?" (Jer 17:9). I know that I long to please the Saviour and have earnestly tried to turn my heart away from every sin. But, surely, as I wait on Him and judge my heart in the light of the Scriptures, God will reveal to me that some matter has lain in my heart, some wicked self-will, some human pride, some critical heart toward others, some failure in prayer, some wavering of faith, which is sin, and which has been sin in my heart so long. Oh, the blind wickedness of the heart of even the best Christian who ever lived! And I am far from the best.

So, according to Scripture, we *now* (present tense) have sin. All of us have sin in our hearts and lives. If we say we have not we are simply deceiving ourselves. To say that we have no sin is not the truth.

We need to read again the indictment against the whole human race given in Romans 3:9-12. Remember, that speaks about me and speaks about you and about every other person who lives on this earth.

> What then? are we better than they? No, in no wise: for we have before proved both Jews and Gentiles, that they are all under sin; As it is written, There is none righteous, no, not one: there is none that understandeth, there is none that seeketh after God. They are all gone out of the

way, they are together become unprofitable; there is none that doeth good, no, not one.

Are we better than others? No, we are sinners. Are you a Jew? Paul has proved "that they are all under sin." Are you a Gentile? Then Paul has proved "that they are all under sin." All the Jews and all the Gentiles are sinners and are under sin.

God says *all*. God means *all*. That means Christians as well as lost sinners. God says not that all *once* were under sin, but that "they all *are* under sin." Now, we Christians and everybody else who lives on the earth in the flesh are under sin.

Again the Scripture says, "There is none righteous, no, not one." How many are righteous in their natural lives? Not one! "No, not one"! It is true that we are counted righteous for Jesus' sake, but that righteousness is His and we cannot speak of our own selves, our own natures, our own thoughts and works as being righteous. We are not.

A rich young ruler came to Jesus and asked Him, "Good Master, what good thing shall I do, that I may have eternal life?" (Mt 19:16). He made two mistakes. First, he wanted to do some good thing to earn eternal life by his works. That was a terrible mistake. His other mistake was that he addressed Jesus as "Good Master," meaning teacher or rabbi. With holy indignation, Jesus very properly answered him, "Why callest thou me good? There is none good but one, that is, God." If Jesus is simply and only a teacher, a rabbi, He is not good. If you say that Jesus is good, then you must set Him apart from all the rest of the human race and you must admit that He is God come in the flesh. But aside from Jesus Christ, not a single person in the world is good. The rest of us are sinners!

Every Christian Has Two Natures—the Old Sinful Nature and the New Divine Nature

Every lost person is born once, born of the flesh, is carnal, human, sinful by nature. Every saved person is born twice and so has two natures, the old nature and the new nature. The old nature is represented by our bodies which still have in them the seed of death and the marks of decay. But the new nature is born of God.

One gets a new heart, or nature, when he is born of God. When Jesus returns, the body, too, will be changed, the fleshly nature also will be adopted, redeemed, and we shall be manifested even physically as sons of God.

Every Christian has a struggle between these two natures, the old nature and the new nature. In Romans 7:15-25 Paul tells of the conflict of the two natures.

> For that which I do I allow not: for what I would, that do I not; but what I hate, that do I. If then I do that which I would not, I consent unto the law that it is good. Now then it is no

more I that do it, but sin that dwelleth in me. For
I know that in me (that is, in my flesh,) dwelleth
no good thing: for to will is present with me; but
how to perform that which is good I find not. For
the good that I would I do not: but the evil which
I would not, that I do. Now if I do that I would
not, it is no more I that do it, but sin that dwelleth in me. I find then a law, that, when I would
do good, evil is present with me. For I delight
in the law of God after the inward man: but I see
another law in my members, warring against the
law of my mind, and bringing me into captivity
to the law of sin which is in my members. O
wretched man that I am! Who shall deliver me
from the body of this death? I thank God through
Jesus Christ our Lord. So then with the mind I
myself serve the law of God; but with the flesh
the law of sin.

Let us approach this Scripture with an honest
heart. Throughout the passage Paul uses the present tense. When he, by divine inspiration, wrote
this passage to the church at Rome, it was then presently true in his own life. Some good people try to
get away from the clear teaching of Romans 7. They
do not like to admit that they, too, still have this
wicked, sinful, carnal nature which is enmity
against God. And so some people teach that chapter 7 of Paul's letter to the Romans represented an
early period in Paul's Christian life when he was
not filled with the Spirit and when he did not have

victory. They say that chapter 8 represents his mature and triumphant Christian life after he had passed through the struggle and no more had the conflict which chapter 7 describes. But they are wrong. Dr. C. I. Scofield errs when he says:

> Just when the apostle passed through the experience of Rom. 7:7-25 we are not told. . . . It is the experience of a renewed man, under the law, and still ignorant of the delivering power of the Holy Spirit. . . . Romans 7 is the record of past conflicts and defeats experienced as a renewed man under law.*

Dr. Scofield says *past* conflicts; Paul says *present* conflicts. He said, "For that which *I do I* allow not: for what I would, that *do I not;* but what I hate, *that do I*." The very day Paul, by divine inspiration, wrote this letter to the Romans, he was compelled to admit that he still had the old nature, still had the conflict, still had to buffet his body and fleshly nature. He still had to confess that "to will is present with me; but how to perform that which is good I find not" (7:18). In verse 25 he says, "So then with the mind I myself serve [present tense] the law of God; but with the flesh the law of sin."

Romans 7 and 8 were written with the same pen, at the same sitting, under the same divine inspiration, and both chapters represented Paul as a mature, Spirit-filled, Christian man. It is never right

*Scofield Bible footnote.

13

to tell people to "get out of the seventh chapter of Romans and into the eighth chapter." It is foolish to cast reflection on the blessed truth of any part of the Bible. It is well to rejoice that we have the new nature. But it is only honest to admit that we also have the old nature and that the one is opposed to the other. Paul had "the law of my mind [or heart]" which was good, and he had "the law of sin which is in my members" (v. 23), which was bad. Paul had the mind or heart to serve the Law of God, but he had the flesh and the fleshly nature to continually tug toward sin.

This twofold nature of the Christian is taught further in 1 John 3:6-9. Read it prayerfully.

> Whosoever abideth in him sinneth not: whosoever sinneth hath not seen him, neither known him. Little children, let no man deceive you: he that doeth righteousness is righteous, even as he is righteous. He that committeth sin is of the devil; for the devil sinneth from the beginning. For this purpose the Son of God was manifested, that he might destroy the works of the devil. Whosoever is born of God doth not commit sin; for his seed remaineth in him: and he cannot sin, because he is born of God.

Here are startling statements: "Whosoever sinneth hath not seen him, neither known him" (v. 6). "He that committeth sin is of the devil" (v. 8). "Whosoever is born of God doth not commit sin;

14

for his seed remaineth in him: and he cannot sin, because he is born of God" (v. 9).

All these statements say that (in the sense meant in this passage) a certain kind of person never sins at all, even *cannot* sin. Does this mean that anybody who ever sins thereby proves he has never known God, has never been saved? No, this means that the new nature, the born-again nature, the new heart of the converted man cannot sin. The old man sins but the new man does not sin, cannot sin.

Charles B. Williams translates these passages, "No one who practices sin has ever seen Him or come to know Him," and "Whoever practices sin belongs to the devil," and "No one who is born of God makes a practice of sinning." This, I believe, not only overstrains the tense of the Greek verb, but teaches something not true. Christian people sometimes *do* practice sin.

Would you say that one who regularly attends the movies and has his mind defiled with the lewdness of Hollywood films does not practice sin? I have known Christians to carry grudges for weeks and months, unforgiveness in the heart. And every day they sin against God. Could you honestly say that such Christians did not practice sin?

Lot stayed in Sodom, we suppose, for years, and all the time the wickedness around him, as he was yoked up with unbelievers, putting money-making first, "vexed his righteous soul" (2 Pe 2:8). Would you say that Lot did not practice sin when he stayed in that city all the years, and never won a soul, never even won any of his own family? It would be right to say that no Christian can continue *happy* in sin.

No Christian can continue in sin without rebuke and without chastisement. But it is not correct and it is not scriptural to say that no Christian practices sin.

No, what God is saying here is that the new nature does not sin. The part that is born of God does not sin. Our bodies, our fleshly natures, are not yet transformed. But they will be.

An Indian was converted, but he had a good deal of struggle to live right. Tapping himself on the breast, he said to the missionary, "Two dogs all the time fighting in here. One is a black dog, a bad dog. One is a white dog, a good dog. They fight all the time."

The missionary explained that one who is born of God has the new nature, but that he also has the fleshly nature to contend with and to overcome. Then he asked the Indian convert, "Which dog wins in the fight?"

"The one I say 'sic 'em' to," was the discerning answer. Thank God, a Christian can live daily in victory over his old self, over his carnal nature. He can confess his sins, can mortify the deeds of the flesh and thus, by walking in the light, can have constant fellowship with God. But he must not ignore the fact of his sinful nature, and he certainly should not deceive himself in thinking that he has no sin or that he does no sin. For all of us do sin.

Thanks be to God, a great time is coming when we will have the rest of our salvation. Now we have only the firstfruits.

In Romans 8 the Holy Spirit speaks of the flesh and the Spirit as being opposed in the Christian. And the old nature is called the flesh, or the creature. In Romans 8:18-23 Paul tells of the wonderful time when we shall receive the rest of our salvation, when the body itself shall be redeemed and adopted, and we shall be outwardly, as well as inwardly, manifest as the sons of God.

> For I reckon that the sufferings of this present time are not worthy to be compared with the glory which shall be revealed in us. For the earnest expectation of the creature waiteth for the manifestation of the sons of God. For the creature was made subject to vanity, not willingly, but by reason of him who hath subjected the same in hope. Because the creature itself also shall be delivered from the bondage of corruption into the glorious liberty of the children of God. For we know that the whole creation groaneth and travaileth in pain together until now. And not only they, but ourselves also, which have the firstfruits of the Spirit, even we ourselves groan within ourselves, waiting for the adoption, to wit, the redemption of our body.

17

Those of us who are saved already have the new heart. One of these glorious days, when Jesus comes, we will have the new body also! Now our bodies and our fleshly natures are unredeemed. We have the frailties of sin in our bodies and the frailties of sin in our natures. We struggle against them. By God's daily help, we can live triumphantly over them. But one day, thank God, we shall be relieved of this conflict, and our old nature shall be changed as we have already been changed in heart and mind. Hallelujah!

Meanwhile, we Christians must honestly admit that sin dwells in us, that we are sinners saved by God's grace.

Bible Christians Sinned as We Do

Let us consider the examples of some Christians of Bible times who, though truly born again, sinned from day to day.

We must remember that everybody who was ever saved was saved the same way—by faith in Christ. God has always had just one way of saving sinners. Those who were saved in the Old Testament times were saved by faith in the coming Saviour. Those who are saved now are saved by faith in the Saviour who has already come. "Abraham believed God and it was counted to him for righteousness." So, we today are saved by simple faith, like Abraham's faith.

Lot was a Christian man. That is made clear from 2 Peter 2:7-9. We are told how God turned the cities of Sodom and Gomorrah into ashes, "And delivered just Lot, vexed with the filthy conversation of the wicked: (For that righteous man dwelling among them, in seeing and hearing, vexed his righteous soul from day to day with their unlawful deeds;) The Lord knoweth how to deliver the godly out of temptations, and to reserve the unjust unto the day of judgment to be punished."

Consider this man Lot. God calls him "just Lot." God calls him "that righteous man." God says that he had a "righteous soul." Then in this case we are told that the "Lord knoweth how to deliver the godly out of temptations." Lot is called a godly man. He was a Christian man.

Yet, Lot is an example of a worldly Christian. He put money and business ahead of serving the Lord. He moved toward Sodom, then into Sodom. He failed to win his wife, his children, his sons-in-law. He failed to win the men of Sodom. He called the wicked "brethren." Lot sinned day by day.

He had a new nature, and the new nature was always grieved at the sin about him. But Lot sinned by staying in Sodom and failing to win souls and by living a worldly life.

David, too, is a tragic example of a man who sinned after he was saved. He was not only saved, a man after God's own heart (1 Sa 13:14) and made

19

king of Israel, but he was inspired to write many of the wonderful psalms in our Bible. Yet, David fell into grossest sin. He led the wife of Uriah, Bathsheba, into adultery and then had Uriah killed to cover up his sin. David suffered terribly for his sins. His baby died under the hand of God; Tamar, his daughter, was raped by a half brother, Amnon. Then Absalom killed Amnon. Then Absalom tried to steal the throne and was killed. What a price David paid for his sin! God chastens every Christian who sins, yet Christians do sin, even as David did.

Peter sinned, too. He cursed and swore and denied the Saviour. He quit the ministry and went back to the fishing business. Then, long after, Peter sinned by compromising the truth, and Paul needed to rebuke him openly, to his face, because he dissembled and "walked not uprightly according to the truth of the gospel" (Gal 2:11-14). But Peter was a saved man.

Every one of these men had the two natures. With the old nature Lot stayed in Sodom, made money, and let his family and the town go to hell. But the new nature within him rebuked him continually. He "vexed his righteous soul from day to day with their unlawful deeds" (2 Pe 2:8). David sinned, but his heartbroken cry for forgiveness in Psalm 51 shows how desperately his heart wanted to do right, and how sorry he was for his sin. The old nature leads a Christian into sin, but the new nature never lets a Christian be happy in sin.

When he cursed and swore and denied the Saviour, Peter committed a terrible sin. Many of us would have judged him, would have said that he was not saved, that he was a hypocrite. Oh, but if we could only see him in that gray dawn of the morning when he heard the rooster crow and then looked at Jesus and went out and wept bitterly, we would realize that here was a man who had the new nature and that the new nature was grieved and shocked at sin and that he bitterly repented of it.

THERE ARE MANY PROOFS THAT ALL CHRISTIANS SIN

Do you need further proofs that you sin? Here they are.

For one thing, all Christians still have a poor, frail, sinful body. The wages of sin is death, and everybody who dies proves that men are sinners. Gray hair, failing eyesight, brittle bones, and disease are all the marks of sin. The perfect angels of God do not have these afflictions. Nor will we have these marks of sin after our bodies are redeemed and we are done with sin.

Jesus taught us in the Lord's Prayer to pray daily for forgiveness. He said we should daily ask, "Forgive us our sins" (Lk 11:4). That proves that all of us are sinners who need daily forgiveness. In the words of 1 John 1:8, "If we say that we have no sin,

we deceive ourselves, and the truth is not in us."
All Christians sin.

We are commanded, "Pray without ceasing" (1 Th 5:17). Everyone sins who is not constantly in unceasing prayer.

The dearest thing to the heart of God is soul-winning. It was to save souls that Jesus came into the world. He gives to everyone of us the Great Commission to take the Gospel to every creature. So everybody who does not win souls is guilty of continued sin.

The Scripture defines sin thus: "Whatsoever is not of faith is sin" (Ro 14:23). Every doubtful thing is sin. Everything one does, about which he has not full assurance that it is in the will of God, is sin. Christians sin!

Again, the Scripture defines sin thus: "To him that knoweth to do good, and doeth it not, to him it is sin" (Ja 4:17). Every Christian sins who has not done as much praying as it would be good to do. Every Christian who does not read the Bible as much as he knows would be best, thereby sins. Every Christian sins who falls short of the glory of God in any manner.

Certainly if we would have the scriptural attitude in the matter we must humbly confess that the Bible is right when it says, "If we say that we have no sin, we deceive ourselves, and the truth is not in us."

2

ONLY GOD'S GRACE CAN KEEP SUCH FRAIL CHRISTIANS SAVED

SIN HAS SO PERVERTED the whole of our natures that only God's grace can save such sinners as we are. And only God's grace can keep such sinners, too. It takes a wonderful salvation to save such sinners as we are. And it takes the same wonderful salvation to keep us.

The Bible doctrine of sin is the foundation of all theology. I do not wonder that God, in infinite wisdom, put the story of man's utter Fall into sin, and the curse that came upon the whole human race and, in fact, upon all creation, because of sin, right in the first part of the Bible. Modernists do not believe that sinners need to be born again because they are not willing to confess that they are, by nature, such infinitely wicked sinners as could be kept out of hell only by the grace of God and the imputed righteousness of Christ!

Those who do not believe in an eternal hell of torment for Christ-rejecting sinners simply do not know how black is the natural human heart, how guilty and deserving of punishment is every sinner who rejects Christ, how incurably wicked are such hearts.

SAVED BY GRACE MEANS KEPT BY GRACE

Thousands of Christians speak glibly of being "saved by grace," but they often mean grace plus something else. I know preachers who say they believe in salvation by grace, but who really believe that one cannot have this grace except by being baptized by immersion by one of their own preachers, by attending services every Lord's Day, taking Communion every Lord's Day, then obeying Christ "in every thought, word and deed" throughout their lives! What a mockery to teach a salvation by works, but to call it salvation by grace!

So many Christians claim to be saved by grace, but they say that this grace can only be kept by working hard for it, "holding out faithful." They have not understood salvation by grace. And they have not understood the clear Bible doctrine of how wicked, how incurably, insatiably wicked is the carnal nature, self-deceived and deceiving others, so that a lost sinner can never deserve salvation to get it. A saved sinner can never deserve salvation to keep it!

Since every Christian still has the old nature, and

since every Christian sins, whether or not he is conscious of any known sin, he is still deceiving himself if he says that he has no sin (1 Jn 1:8). Since every Christian is commanded to pray daily, "Forgive us our sins" (Lk 11:4), then we conclude that God Himself must provide a salvation that includes His own perfect righteousness given freely to the undeserving sinner!

If God, by divine grace, by unmerited favor, can change the heart of a poor sinner and give him a new heart, make him a child of God, a partaker of the divine nature, then God must also provide for the saving by grace of the old man also, the redemption of our bodies and our carnal natures, too!

God forbade a Jew to wear a garment of linen and wool together or to plow with an ox and an ass together (Deu 22:10-11). God forbade the yoking of believer and unbeliever, the saved and the lost, in marriage and otherwise. But none of these yokes could be as unequal as the yoke some people imagine exists between a salvation that is supposedly given free for only a moment by God's grace, but then must be kept during all the following years by human works! The man who is incapable of saving himself is equally incapable of keeping himself.

I did not deserve salvation when I received it years ago, a nine-year-old boy at Gainesville, Texas. It would have served me right if God had let me go on my own wicked way to land in hell. Now, even after I am saved, I must admit that there have never been thirty seconds of my life in which I have deserved salvation. When I have done all that I can do, I am properly commanded to say that I am an unprofitable servant (Lk 17:10). If God does not have a way of keeping poor, undeserving sinners who cannot earn today's salvation, who cannot earn the resurrection of the body, who cannot earn the redemption of this old nature, then I am undone! But thanks be to God, He who saved by grace also keeps by grace. Thank God, the One who gave the firstfruits of our redemption when we received a new heart, when the Holy Spirit came in to dwell, will now do the rest of the blessed job of salvation by the same grace. "Being confident of this very thing, that he which hath begun a good work in you will perform it until the day of Jesus Christ" (Phil 1:6).

THE BELIEVER HAS COUNTED TO HIM THE RIGHTEOUSNESS OF CHRIST

How clear this wonderful plan of salvation is made in Romans 4, which tells us how Abraham, the father of the believing, was saved.

> What shall we say then that Abraham our father, as pertaining to the flesh, hath found? For if Abraham were justified by works, he hath whereof to glory; but not before God. For what saith the scripture? Abraham believed God, and

26

it was counted unto him for righteousness. Now to him that worketh is the reward not reckoned of grace, but of debt. But to him that worketh not, but believeth on him that justifieth the ungodly, his faith is counted for righteousness. Even as David also describeth the blessedness of the man, unto whom God imputeth righteousness without works, saying, Blessed are they whose iniquities are forgiven, and whose sins are covered. Blessed is the man to whom the Lord will not impute sin (Ro 4:1-8).

Here we are told that Abraham was not justified by works. If he had been justified by works he would have something to boast of, but not before God. If Abraham was saved by his good works, then he would have no right to talk about the blood, about the Saviour, about redemption, about God's grace. But "Abraham believed God, and it was counted unto him for righteousness."

Then we are told, "Now to him that worketh is the reward not reckoned of grace, but of debt." No one has a right to call it salvation by grace if he has earned it. If any man could say, "This day I have kept myself in the grace of God; this day I have worked for God and I have deserved His blessing," then that man should not talk about the grace of God. He and God are on an equal plane. He has earned good things from God, and God must give them. But God would then be just paying honest debts, not giving salvation by grace. No, grace and works are mutually exclusive. No one has the right to talk about God's grace while he depends upon his own goodness.

Now notice wonderful verse 5: "But to him that worketh not, but believeth on him that justifieth the ungodly, his faith is counted for righteousness." We are plainly told that one who is saved "worketh not." A sinner cannot do a single thing to earn credit with God! Also, we learn the startling fact that God "justifieth the ungodly." It is not the godly whom God justifieth, but the ungodly! If God did not furnish the godliness free, no one could be saved. But this ungodly sinner may trust in Christ and have his faith counted for righteousness.

Then we have that wonderful promise quoted from Psalm 32, in Romans 4:6-8:

> Even as David also describeth the blessedness of the man, unto whom God imputeth righteousness without works, saying, Blessed are they whose iniquities are forgiven, and whose sins are covered. Blessed is the man to whom the Lord will not impute sin.

Here we are plainly told that the poor lost sinner simply receives the righteousness of Christ. This righteousness is put to his credit. God counts this righteousness to the man "without works," and then the sinner is one of those blessed ones whose iniquities are forgiven and whose sins are covered. Every believing, trusting sinner, then, is the blessed man "to whom the Lord will not impute sin." That is being saved by grace and being kept by grace!

Again in Romans 1:3-4 we are plainly told of the great mistake of the Jews.

> For they being ignorant of God's righteousness, and going about to establish their own righteousness, have not submitted themselves unto the righteousness of God. For Christ is the end of the law for righteousness to every one that believeth.

Thank God, since I came to trust Jesus the whole Law of God is counted kept. All the righteousness of Christ is counted as mine. All my sins, once and forever, are nailed to the cross of Jesus Christ. All the sins before I was saved, all the sins after I was saved, are laid on Jesus. Jesus paid the whole price at one time. His righteousness is now my righteousness, and His standing before God is my standing before God!

How else could such sinners as we are, ever be kept for heaven when "the heart is deceitful above all things, and desperately wicked: who can know it?" (Jer 17:9). Then how could I even know my sins well enough, day by day, to confess them and forsake them surely and completely? And even "when I would do good, evil is present with me" (Ro 7:21), and again, "for to will is present with me; but how to perform that which is good I find not" (7:18). When I realize the wretchedness of this old nature which makes it easier to do wrong than to do right, easier to play than to work for God, easier to be at ease than to be in earnest, heart-broken prayer, easier to go along with the world rather than to stem the tide and stand true to God at any cost, I must cry with Paul, "O wretched man that I am! Who shall deliver me from the body of this death?" But I can also give the same divine answer that Paul gave, "I thank God through Jesus Christ our Lord" (Ro 7:24-25). Yes, since "with the mind I myself serve the law of God; but with the flesh the law of sin" (v. 25), I must have divine righteousness given me freely. I must have salvation not of my works. I must be kept by the power of God. Thank God, that is the kind of salvation, the kind of keeping that every Christian has!

3

WHAT SIN DOES TO THE CHRISTIAN

SOME PEOPLE who make a very easy and glib claim of "entire sanctification" and who say that they are in that wonderful state of "perfect love," in which they do no sin, berate some of us who preach much on salvation by grace. They say that we "encourage sin." They say that we preach "a sinning religion."

No, no! I do not encourage sin. I must solemnly tell every Christian who reads this that sin is a fearful matter. It brings unnumbered woes and troubles! Sin never paid anybody. It is the most hateful thing, the most to be feared, the most to be despised in all the universe of God! I do not encourage people to sin. With all my soul I plead with Christians everywhere to flee from sin, to judge sin, to search their hearts daily to confess and forsake sin.

I do not encourage sin. That is one reason I plead with those who foolishly deceive themselves. Some people will play down every sin and call it simply "a mistake." They fail God in soul-winning, they fail God in prayer, they omit to do the things they know they should do, thus they sin. But they call such errors simply "mistakes." They hush the voice of conscience. They have little compunction when they do not win souls. They blatantly boast of how much better they are than many other Christians, and yet in their boasting see no sin. I do not encourage sin. I simply insist that it is wrong to lie about it and wrong to pretend a godlike state of perfection which we do not have. Any man who has graying hair, decaying teeth, and evidences of disease, anyone who does not have all the perfection and glory of the pure angels of God, the glory which redeemed saints will have in heaven, should know that he grieves God all the more by his foolish claims when he fails to confess his sin daily, as Jesus commanded us to do.

Sin brings terrible loss and punishment and pain. Let me name for you some of the things sin brings to a Christian.

SIN BRINGS CHASTISEMENT TO CHRISTIANS

Consider this plain warning in Hebrews 12:4-8:

> Ye have not yet resisted unto blood, striving against sin. And ye have forgotten the exhortation which speaketh unto you as unto children, My son, despise not thou the chastening of the Lord, nor faint when thou art rebuked of him: for whom the Lord loveth he chasteneth, and scourgeth every son whom he receiveth. If ye en-

dure chastening, God dealeth with you as with sons; for what son is he whom the father chasteneth not? But if ye be without chastisement, whereof all are partakers, then are ye bastards, and not sons.

Here God makes a plain statement that every child of God is chastened, and one who does not have chastisement from God is a bastard and not a son (v. 8). But we are plainly told in verse 4 that chastisement comes because of sin, "Ye have not yet resisted unto blood, striving against sin."

Later in the same passage we are told that God chastens us that "we might be partakers of his holiness" (v. 10). Oh, blessed rod of God's chastisement to help purge us from our sins and to make us more fit for heaven and for His presence!

But since every Christian receives such chastisement, then every Christian sins.

The Christians at Corinth had a fellow church member who lived in vile sin. So Paul commanded them:

In the name of our Lord Jesus Christ, when ye are gathered together, and my spirit, with the power of our Lord Jesus Christ, to deliver such an one unto Satan for the destruction of the flesh, that the spirit may be saved in the day of the Lord Jesus (1 Co 5:4-5).

Here a blessed truth is given. Even this man living in terrible sin was a child of God. But he was to be left to punishment "for the destruction of the flesh" in order that "the spirit may be saved in the day of the Lord Jesus." God cannot punish His saints in hell in the next world. The Christian's chastening must come now. Later we learn that this same man, so rebuked and chastened, came in penitence and was received back into fellowship in the church.

Sin brings chastening from God.

What happens to a Christian as God's punishment for his sins? That question is partly answered in 1 Corinthians 11. There Paul addresses the church at Corinth which had had divisions, quarrels, worldliness, a formal and flippant observance of the Lord's Supper, without any judging of sin in their lives. So Paul wrote:

> But let a man examine himself, and so let him eat of that bread, and drink of that cup. For he that eateth and drinketh unworthily, eateth and drinketh damnation to himself, not discerning the Lord's body. For this cause many are weak and sickly among you, and many sleep. For if we would judge ourselves, we should not be judged. But when we are judged, we are chastened of the Lord, that we should not be condemned with the world (1 Co 11:28-32).

The condemnaiton, or damnation, mentioned in verse 29 does not mean condemnation to hell, but

34

condemnation to God's judgment and punishment in this world. Then verse 30 explains, "For this cause many are weak and sickly among you, and many sleep." God had smitten some Christians with disease because of their sins. Others He had taken home to heaven. They had died because of their sins.

We are solemnly warned that every Christian ought to judge himself carefully, lest he should be judged of God and punished. But, thank God, He chastens us instead of letting us be condemned with the world, as lost sinners are condemned to hell!

How many homes have someone who is sick because sin in the Christian has grieved God! It is not always true that our sickness comes because of sin. But sometimes, surely it does. I know that sometimes one may be sick, as was Job, to the glory of God and not because of sin. But we have many warnings that disease and illness may be the chastening of God on His own beloved child.

This is implied in James 5:14-15:

> Is any sick among you? Let him call for the elders of the church; and let them pray over him, anointing him with oil in the name of the Lord: and the prayer of faith shall save the sick, and the Lord shall raise him up; and if he have committed sins, they shall be forgiven him.

Note that "the prayer of faith shall save the sick,

and the Lord shall raise him up; *and if he have committed sins, they shall be forgiven him.*"

Again, note verse 16 which plainly tells those who wish to be healed to "confess your faults one to another, and pray one for another." Often some sin, unjudged, unconfessed, means that God cannot smile upon us and give us the blessing of health as He would like to do.

How many, many times the Bible speaks of disease coming as a chastisement of God. When Miriam opposed her brother Moses, she was smitten with leprosy. King Uzziah, who intruded into the priest's office and offered sacrifices, received the same dread curse in his body and was a leper until the day of his death. Gehazi, the servant of Elisha who secretly received the garments and the gift of money after Naaman the Syrian was healed, was stricken with leprosy for his avarice.

Sometimes a Christian died prematurely because of his sin. That happened to some of those at Corinth. Paul said, "For this cause many are weak and sickly among you, *and many sleep*" (1 Co 11:30). Some of the Corinthian Christians who were careless about the Lord's Supper, even getting drunk and making divisions in the church, had been called home to heaven.

You remember that Ananias and Sapphira lied to the Holy Spirit about money and were killed. The Bible does not say that they were lost people; they may have been really born-again Christians. But they died for their sins.

Even the mighty Moses, the lawgiver, because once in a crucial time he lost his temper and did not give glory to God, was not allowed to go into the promised land but was taken to Mount Nebo and died there. God loved him and took him home to heaven, but his death was premature, brought on, as God plainly told Moses, by his sin. (See Num 20:12; Deu 32:49-51.)

I am sure that I have seen God take some of His own children to heaven prematurely because of their sin. Once in a young church, greatly blessed of God with many souls being saved, several men, in order to get control and leadership in the church, joined enemies of the pastor in a conspiracy. One of the most active men fell dead of a heart attack. Another was rushed to the hospital with some strange malady and in a few hours was dead, the cause of his sickness unknown. Another of the men went to the hospital and was dead in two or three days. A fourth one was in an airplane accident and suddenly killed. I have every reason to believe that these men were saved men, but that sin and self-will led them far wrong and that God took them home, as He did some of the Christians at Corinth, because of their sins.

We are clearly warned that if we do not judge our own sins, God will judge them and punish them.

The heavy hand of God falls on unconfessed, unlamented, unrepented sin in a Christian!

How often must God reach down and take a baby home to heaven before the mother and father will listen and turn from their worldliness!

Do you remember how the chastening hand of God fell on David's baby, the baby which Bathsheba conceived in sin? Despite all David's praying, the baby died. The child died as punishment. The prophet of God said, "Howbeit, because by this deed thou hast given great occasion to the enemies of the LORD to blaspheme, the child also that is born unto thee shall surely die." Then we are told, "And the LORD struck the child that Uriah's wife bare unto David, and it was very sick" (2 Sa 12:14-15). The terrible, inexorable, dreadful hand of God struck David's child and the child died! Thus, we learn how God sometimes chastens His children with the death of loved ones.

In a blessed tent ervival campaign in Roosevelt, Oklahoma, one night, I had preached most plainly on how God speaks to people in chastisement when they sin. A man came to see me after the service. He was holding in his arms a beautiful little girl about two years old. He said to me, "Brother Rice, you are right. I know from sad experience that God punishes His children when they go into sin. This baby girl had a twin brother. He was the dearest, smartest child you ever saw! I loved him almost to the point of worship. But sickness seized the little one and when he died God told me plainly it was because of my sin. I came back to my heavenly Father with confession and have lived much closer to Him since. But God took my baby to bring me to my senses."

I do not wonder that the psalmist David cried out, "Before I was afflicted I went astray" (Ps 119: 67).

Sometimes God brings chastisement by business losses, by lost jobs, by poverty and other sore trouble.

Do you remember how Lot, down in Sodom, a child of God, lost all his property in the fire and brimstone which fell from heaven? He lost his family; his wife was turned to a pillar of salt, his married daughters and sons-in-law and grandchildren were burned to death. But he lost his property, too, in the judgment of God upon sin.

Again and again Christians have told me how they got absorbed in money-making, how they robbed God of tithes and offerings, then some disaster came and God thus collected the gifts that should have been freely given to Him.

In the prophecy of Malachi (Mal 3:9) the Jews are told, "Ye are cursed with a curse: for ye have robbed me, even this whole nation." And he speaks plainly of a curse upon the ground, the crops, the weather. He promises them if they will bring all the tithes into the storehouse that "I will rebuke the devourer for your sakes, and he shall not destroy the fruits of your ground; neither shall your vine cast her fruit before the time in the field, saith the LORD of hosts" (Mal 3:11).

The prophet Haggai rebuked the children of Israel for their sins. He said, "Ye have sown much, and bring in little; ye eat, but ye have not enough; ye drink, but ye are not filled with drink; ye clothe you, but there is none warm; and he that earneth wages earneth wages to put it into a bag with holes" (Hag 1:6). God says plainly that, because His own house is left waste, He has blown upon the crops to destroy them. He stopped the dew from heaven and stopped the earth from her fruit and called for a drought upon the land!

In Deuteronomy 28, it tells of terrible curses that would come upon the land of Israel if they should forsake the Lord their God. God does bring financial disaster, poverty, because of sin. He often brings such trouble even on His own people, Christians, because of sin.

One Saturday night as I took an old German Christian couple to their farm home near Wichita Falls, Texas, we came upon an overturned car. One of the young women was so injured that she later spent weeks in the hospital. All were shaken up, bruised, and scared. I took them to their homes in my car and talked seriously to them about the Lord.

I found that two of them were backsliders. With tears they confessed their backsliding and begged God to forgive them. They felt that the automobile accident was a warning from God and a judgment for their worldly lives. I thought so, too.

I know Christians whose homes have been broken because of sin. I know Christians who, because of their sins, lost the confidence of their children. I know Christians who lost their jobs, who suffered financial disaster, and they are firmly convinced that these things were the chastening hand of God upon them to bring them back from a wayward course that grieved God. God chastises His children when they sin.

Sin Brings the Loss of Christian Joy

Every Christian should be glad all the time. But even a child of God, on his way to heaven, knowing that he is saved, cannot be happy if there be known sin unjudged, unrebuked, and unconfessed in his life.

Sin in the Christian brings the smiting of conscience. It brings the rebuke of the Holy Spirit. No Christian can be a happy Christian, except as he day by day seeks to live in the smile of God's approval. Godly living does not earn salvation, but it does bring happiness.

In Psalm 51 we have the heartbroken prayer of

David after his sin with Bathsheba. There David prayed:

> Make me to hear joy and gladness; that the bones which thou hast broken may rejoice. Hide thy face from my sins, and blot out all mine iniquities. Create in me a clean heart, O God; and renew a right spirit within me. Cast me not away from thy presence; and take not thy holy spirit from me. Restore unto me the joy of thy salvation; and uphold me with thy free spirit. Then will I teach transgressors thy ways; and sinners shall be converted unto thee (Ps 51:8-13).

David had been weeping over his baby who died because of David's sin. He had been weeping over his own lost fellowship with God. He begged for the cleansing of his heart anew, a renewal of a right spirit. He begged for the fellowship of the Holy Spirit. Then he said, "Restore unto me the joy of thy salvation." David had lost the joy of his salvation.

David did not pray, "Restore unto me thy salvation." He prayed, "Restore unto me *the joy* of thy salvation."

David knew that only with cleansing from sin, only by the comfort of the Holy Spirit, only by being upheld and helped to walk straight, could he have the joy which ought to go with salvation. He begged that that joy should be restored. He promised, "Then will I teach transgressors thy ways; and sinners shall be converted unto thee."

How often I have read that blessed Psalm 51 and made its prayer my prayer! How often I have been compelled to say, as did David, "My sin is ever before me" (v. 3). I, too, have had to plead, "Behold, I was shapen in iniquity; and in sin did my mother conceive me" (v. 5). I have such a frail, twisted nature. I am as weak as David. When I sin I lose the joy. So, of course, do you, if you are a born-again Christian. Anyone who claims that he can go into sin and have no burning of conscience, have no unrest of soul, and have no accusing by the Holy Spirit, gives evidence that he does not know the same Saviour I know and does not have the new heart which God gave me when I was saved.

O Christian, I remind you now that sin never made anybody happy. Most of all, sin cannot make the Christian happy. A Christian loses the joy of salvation when he falls into sin.

I do not wonder that Peter "went out, and wept bitterly" (Mt 26:75) after he denied the Saviour. His sin took all his joy. Sin will take away your joy, too, if you allow it for a moment, unjudged, unconfessed in your life.

SIN LOSES MUCH OF THE BLESSED HELP OF THE HOLY SPIRIT IN THE CHRISTIAN'S LIFE

The Holy Spirit lives in every Christian's body.

43

Yet, when a Christian sins he sometimes loses all contact with that same Holy Spirit. It seems as if the Holy Spirit, like an ill-treated and offended guest, shuts Himself up in His own small room in the heart and does not enjoy the fellowship of the inmate who has so grieved Him and wronged Him! The blessed Holy Spirit does not leave when a Christian sins, but His work is certainly hindered.

By sin a Christian may lose the assurance of salvation. In 2 Peter we are told of the virtue, knowledge, temperance, patience, godliness, brotherly kindness, and charity which a Christian should add to his saving faith. Then we are plainly warned, "But he that lacketh these things is blind, and cannot see afar off, and hath forgotten that he was purged from his old sins" (2 Pe 1:9). Often the Christian who does not obey God, who sins in not going on in the full flower and usefulness and growth of the Christian life, "hath forgotten that he was purged from his old sins." How often Christians lose the assurance of salvation because they have lost their joy.

I know it was so in my own case. No one showed me how to know by the Word of God that I had everlasting life. So, when I was discouraged and fell into sin, I thought that God had forsaken me. That comforting voice of the Holy Spirit that told me I was a child of God was silenced, grieved by my sin.

Well did the apostle Peter himself know about

44

this! God doubtless brought to his mind how he, after he denied the Saviour, went out and wept so bitterly, then quit the ministry and went back to the fishing business. He thought he was washed up. He thought that he had no more right to preach the Gospel. Here he reminds us, by divine inspiration, that we too may lose that sweet, comforting assurance that the Holy Spirit gives in our hearts if we let sin go unconfessed and unforsaken.

A Christian May Miss the Leading of the Holy Spirit

It is normal for the blessed Holy Spirit to speak to a Christian day by day and tell him the road he should walk. It is normal for a Christian to have such contact with the Spirit that he can know what to say to a lost sinner he seeks to win, that he may know which invitation to accept and which to reject. A Christian has a right to the help of the Holy Spirit in understanding the Bible, a right to the sweet comfort of the Spirit, a right to the help of the Holy Spirit in prayer. But all these blessed ministries of the Holy Spirit are hindered when we let sin stay and fester in the life unconfessed, unlamented, unforsaken.

In Alexander, Texas, I remember a woman who insisted that she was lost. She had no joy, her prayers were not answered, she had none of that sweet ministration of the Spirit which a Christian has the right to enjoy. Her husband, her father-in-law, her friends were shocked. She had been one of the best Christians they had ever known.

But when I dealt with her I led her bit by bit to see that some sin had grieved God, that she had thus lost the assurance she had once had and the blessed teaching and guidance of the Spirit which are normal and right. Then she knew what had happened. She told me something like this: "I once won many, many souls to Christ. Then I moved into this little town where some people were proud and haughty. I seemed an ignorant country woman. When the Holy Spirit told me to go speak to that woman about her soul, I trembled and refused to go. Again when the Holy Spirit urged me to speak to that boy who came to my door, I did not do it. Again and again the Spirit moved my heart as He had done for years in the past when I obeyed Him. But when I refused and my timidity and seeking to please men led me to disobey the Spirit's leading, the time came when He talked to me no more. I never had another impression to talk to sinners. When I read the Bible I got little light from its pages. When I prayed I did not have the blessed uplift and leading and fervor which the Holy Spirit had given me before. I felt that God had turned His back on me and that I must be lost."

What had happened was that the blessed Holy Spirit was offended by her sin. She had "quenched the Spirit," which we are plainly commanded not to do (1 Th 5:19). She had grieved the Spirit by sin (Eph 4:30). She was still saved. The Holy Spirit still lived in her body. But the blessed fruit which the Spirit gives He could not give her because of rebellion and sin. Oh, what loss for a Christian when sin is made at home and entertained willingly in the life!

A Christian's Sins Can Shut God's Ears Against His Prayers

God delights to hear the prayers of His people. We are told, "He that spared not his own Son, but delivered him up for us all, how shall he not with him also freely give us all things?" (Ro 8:32). We are plainly invited and promised, "Ask, and it shall be given you; seek, and ye shall find; knock, and it shall be opened unto you" (Mt 7:7). The Lord solemnly states that it is simply because we do not keep on asking that we do not have (Ja 4:2). Most Christians live far below the level of joy and usefulness and provision which God intended His children to have, simply because we do not take everything to God in prayer and ask our heavenly Father for what we need. But we are plainly warned that sin shuts up heaven to our prayers.

In Isaiah 59:1-3 read this solemn statement:

> Behold, the LORD's hand is not shortened, that it cannot save; neither his ear heavy, that it can-

not save; neither his ear heavy, that it cannot hear: But your iniquities have separated between you and your God, and your sins have hid his face from you, that he will not hear. For your hands are defiled with blood, and your fingers with iniquity; your lips have spoken lies, your tongue hath muttered perverseness.

Our sins have turned away from us the God who would be so willing to hear if our sins were out of the way.

Another plain Scripture on this matter is Psalm 66:18, which says: "If I regard iniquity in my heart, the Lord will not hear me." Any known sin, unconfessed, unjudged, unforsaken, makes it so that God cannot honorably and righteously give us many of the things we ask for and need. God cannot put Himself in the position of endorsing our sins when He answers the prayers of sinning Christians who do not judge their sins and do not turn from them.

Oh, what confidence, what happy freedom one may have when he approaches God in prayer, knowing that he has solemnly and earnestly taken sides with God against his own sins, that he has judged and rebuked, and turned from every known thing that would grieve the dear Saviour! That is what the Scripture means in 1 John 3:21-22:

Beloved, if our heart condemn us not, then have we confidence toward God. And whatsoever we ask, we receive of him, because we keep his commandments, and do those things that are pleasing in his sight.

Let every reader search his heart. Are you sure there is not a single known sin unconfessed to come to haunt your prayer life, to offend your heavenly Father, to grieve the sweet Spirit of God who dwells within you? O Christian, how sad when our sins shut up heaven against our prayers and make it so God cannot hear as He wants to do!

A Christian's Sin May Bring a Curse upon His Loved Ones

The holy law of a jealous God is this:

> For I the LORD thy God am a jealous God, visiting the iniquity of the fathers upon the children unto the third and fourth generation of them that hate me; and shewing mercy unto thousands of them that love me, and keep my commandments (Ex 20:5-6).

That does not mean that God punishes the innocent who do not deserve punishment. It means that a righteous God, giving man free will and choice, cannot keep children from following in the steps of their worldly and sinful parents. So, when parents sin they bring a curse upon their children. The Christian wife is cursed by the sin of the husband. The moving story of David's great sin and its consequences is illustrative of the curse that comes on others by the sins of a Christian. There can be no doubt that David was a child of God; and in the fact that he was saved and in his general devotion, he is said to have been a man after God's own heart (1 Sa 13:14). Yet, when David sinned, he suffered; and his loved ones suffered, too.

When Nathan told King David the parable of the rich man who robbed his poor neighbor of a little ewe lamb, David in anger said, "As the LORD liveth, the man that hath done this thing shall surely die: and he shall restore the lamb fourfold, because he did this thing, and because he had no pity" (2 Sa 12:5-6). David did not know, but he was pronouncing a righteous judgment on himself. He deserved to die. But Nathan said unto David, "The LORD also hath put away thy sin; thou shalt not die" (2 Sa 12:13). But as David said the stolen lamb must be restored fourfold, so God allowed him to reap fourfold among his own dear ones, the punishment for his sin against Uriah.

First of all, "the LORD struck the child that Uriah's wife bare unto David" (2 Sa 12:15) and the child died as the prophet Nathan had plainly told David. Despite all David's prayers and tears, the little one was taken away.

Again, David's sin appeared in his son Amnon, a spoiled son who consciously, or unconsciously, went into the same kind of sin that David committed. He raped his own half sister Tamar. David, do you weep for the shame on your beautiful daughter who goes home to her brother Absalom's house with her garments torn and with earth upon her head, wringing her hands? But David, this is only twofold, and speaking as a prophet you said, "He shall restore the lamb fourfold" (2 Sa 12:6). The curse has not departed from David's house!

Next, Absalom bided his time and eventually hired his servants to strike Amnon with the dagger of vengeance. A son of David died in disgrace. David first follows the little baby carried to the cemetery with tears, then considers his beautiful daughter ruined. But David, this is only threefold! The lamb must be restored fourfold! The curse has not departed from David's house.

Absalom himself rebelled against King David, seized the kingdom, and sought his father's life. At a price of war and bloodshed the rebellion was put down, and Absalom died with arrows through his breast, hung from his hair in the branches of an oak! David paid fourfold for his sin. But, oh, remember that his loved ones paid, too! There is a curse upon the family of the Christian who sins.

The sins of a pastor may curse his people. I knew well one preacher of great ability who was, I think, for a season, greatly used of God. But a moral decay set in in his life, and I can trace in the lives of a hundred other preachers the disastrous results of the arrogant pride, the boasting, the lying, of the preacher who sins.

A Sunday school teacher may, by compromise or sin, bring a curse upon little children. The Sunday school teacher who attends the movies may explain in great detail that she selects the movies very carefully and attends only the best. But her pupils only know that she puts her endorsement upon Hollywood, upon the commercial picture show, and they will want to go. They will say, "Mother, my Sunday school teacher thinks it's all right; she goes to the movies. Why can't I go?"

Dr. J. Wilbur Chapman told of the influence of a Sunday school teacher who taught her Sunday school class to play cards:

> While a friend of mine was conducting a meeting one morning, a tramp came in and said, "My father and mother used to sit in this pew. It is the first church I ever attended. My father was an officer in this church. Seven boys used to sit in this pew in the Sunday School class. We had a great love and respect for our Sunday School teacher. Saturday afternoon she invited us to her home, entertaining with music, eatables, and a look over the lesson. After a while she was anxious to please us and hold us, and she taught us the names of cards. None had ever used cards. We became enthusiastic over it, learning different games. After a while we would not give so much time to the lesson, but she let us have more time for playing

52

cards, and would show us some more tricks. After a while we were off in the cotton gins playing cards and not going to her home. Later we failed to go to Sunday School. Cards, cigarettes, after a while drink and gambling. We all at different times left our homes. Two of those boys have been hung, three are in state prisons for life, one a vagabond like myself. No one knows where he is and if the authorities knew I was here, I would be arrested and put behind the bars. All I wish is that that teacher had never taught us how to play cards."

As he stood there brokenhearted, a lady at the right and near the pulpit, dressed in mourning arose, went to where the man was, fell on the floor with a scream, and said, "My God! I am the Sunday School teacher that did it." She fainted and we did not know but that she was dead. She revived. The woman was not seen any more in the meeting and the man never seen since.

Every Christian who falls into sin should know that his influence will drag others down, that his powerlessness may prove a curse to others, that his failure may be a blight in spreading disease among those who know him and love him. Oh, how a Christian should hate and fear sin!

Sin Takes away the Soul-Winning Passion and Power of a Christian

As a Christian gives way to sin in his life, he loses

both the desire and the power to win souls. Sin makes a coward of the Christian so that he dare not plead with sinners to be saved. Sin dulls his conscience so that he does not much care. Worse still, sin so grieves the Spirit of God that one cannot have His fullness, His mighty power, except in genuine heart-turning away from sin and in obedience to Christ.

A sad example of such a powerless Christian is Lot down in Sodom. If he had won nine of his own family the city would have been spared and others would have had a chance to be saved. But Lot could not win his own wife, could not win his daughters, could not win his sons-in-laws. He was "as one that mocked unto his sons in law" (Gen 19:14). Souls go to hell because Christians sin. Revivals fail to come because Christians sin. The moral revolution that we need in our homes, our cities, our churches, our nation does not come because of the sins of Christians. Heaven is shut up to our prayers and the winning of precious souls diminishes because Christian people do not turn from their sins. Oh, sin, *sin!* What a price any Christian pays to entertain you in his heart and life! How unconfessed sins, unjudged sins, unforsaken sins blight the life and influence of a Christian.

Every Spirit-filled minister has been grieved to see some Christians lose their soul-winning power and soul-winning joy. Sometimes whole churches lose their concern for sinners. Usually such backslidden Christians do not admit their backsliding. They rationalize their lack of soul-winning power. Some preachers say that they are called to do Bible teaching, not evangelism, when in truth sin has taken away their power as well as their concern for sinners. Whole churches get to where the Gospel invitation to openly accept Christ and claim Him publicly is never given, because sin has taken away the passion for souls. Worldliness creeps in and crowds out the holy zeal which God gives His children who stay near the cross.

The relationship between sin in a Christian and the loss of soul-winning concern and power is known to every successful, God-anointed evangelist. Technical theologians who deal in abstract theories try to separate between a revival and evangelism. They insist that an evangelistic campaign should not be called a revival. They say that revival is for Christians only, and that evangelism is for lost people only. How foolish to try to separate what God has joined together! The simple truth is that no one will ever have a great ingathering of lost people unless, first of all, God deals with His own people, the saved, and gives them a new sensitiveness toward sin, a new cleansing by the blood, and a new passion and concern for lost people about them.

Often people have criticized evangelists because they preached for a week or two to Christian people getting Christians ready to pray and ready to win souls. Some have complained that evangelists do wrong to denounce sin among Christians. They say that evangelists should simply preach the plan of salvation and leave the reviving of Christians to the pastors. But all greatly used evangelists know that the ministry of the evangelist is, first of all, to the saints of God to get them cleansed and reenlisted in the soul-winning business. The evangelist who will win multitudes of souls must rekindle in the Christian's heart the fires of holy concern which have been smothered out by coldness, indifference, worldliness, carelessness, lukewarmness, and sometimes coarser sin.

That leads me to say that pastors are foolish who lament the powerlessness of churches and the lack of fruitfulness among their members, if they do not boldly denounce sin. Pastors ought to be against sin because it is sin and hateful to God, an enemy of the Gospel. But the evangelistic church must keep a sharp, bold testimony against sin. The sinning, worldly, compromising Christian cannot maintain the passion and burden which enable him to win souls. The wayward Christian cannot have the power of God nor the zeal of God. O pastors, "Preach the word; be instant in season, out of season; reprove, rebuke, exhort with all longsuffering and doctrine" (2 Ti 4:2).

THE SINS OF CHRISTIANS BRING A REPROACH
ON CHRIST AND THE BIBLE

One of the worst things that the sin of a Christian does is to bring a reproach on the cause of Christ and upon the name of Christ. How Jerusalem must have buzzed with gossip when Peter denied the Lord, cursed and swore and quit the ministry!

When David committed his great sin, Nathan said, "Howbeit, because by this deed thou hast given great occasion to the enemies of the LORD to blaspheme, the child also that is born unto thee shall surely die" (2 Sa 12:14). The sins of the preacher who falls are blazoned on the front pages of newspapers. The sins of a simple lay Christian are held up in his own family and in his own community against Christ and the Gospel by those who are the enemies of God. What shame and reproach the failure and sins of God's people bring on the whole cause of Christ!

Sometime ago an atheistic publishing house sent me a book mocking the Bible and the Christian religion. The book was full of cartoons and ribald stories about the incest of Lot, about the adultery and murder which David committed, about the shame of Samson and Delilah. The centuries have come and gone. These men who wept over their sins have come to God for forgiveness and have been forgiven. Now they have long since been received into heaven by God's infinite grace, which saves sinners and covers their sin with the precious blood of Christ. But the centuries have not stopped the shameful reproach on the cause of Christ, brought by the sins of these men! The offense may be and has been forgiven in God's loving mercy. But the hateful effects of the sin go on!

I have visited countless churches where some of the most earnest Christians had a sad past. In past years they had fallen into sin. The home was broken by divorce. The scandal was in the newspapers. Later the divorced couple went on to marry other mates. Then, turning to the Lord, they received forgiveness. In many such cases the past cannot be undone. The former marriage is broken and cannot be restored. To break the second marriage by another divorce, another public scandal, is not commanded in the Bible and would do harm and not good. Often there is simply no way to undo the past, whether it is a murder victim who cannot be brought back to life, a home broken which cannot be restored, a crime committed which has brought public shame and which cannot be lived down. I advise such Christians to patiently face criticism with humility and confession. I advise them to patiently serve the Lord in the smallest places, without seeking leadership, until by years of faithfulness, they prove themselves worthy of greater trust. Every pastor knows, also every evangelist, that sins in the past of countless Christians rise up to mock the Church and to give Jesus Christ reproach before the world! How sad that God's cause suffers because His children have sinned! How sad that every evangelist who would lead in a blessed revival campaign finds his efforts hindered by the public reproach brought on the Gospel message by Church people! Oh, God must punish the sins of His own children because of the heartbreaking reproach that sin brings to His dear cause!

4

THE CHRISTIAN'S HAPPINESS IN HEAVEN DEPENDS ON HOW HE LIVED ON EARTH

AGAIN LET ME SAY that I do not encourage sin. No one must treat sin lightly. We are not soon done with the disaster of sin. The Christian who sins will suffer for it in this life. He will suffer for it in the life to come.

Some people suppose that every sinner who goes to heaven will have the same joy and happiness. But that is not true. In Revelation 20, we find that sinners who go to hell are judged, every man according to his works, according to the things written down in God's books. The torment of unsaved people in hell will differ, each one according to his opportunity and according to his sin.

Likewise, the Bible makes it abundantly clear that not all Christians will enjoy the same position and have the same honor and responsibility and blessing in heaven. It is true that each one who trusts in Christ has the same salvation and goes to the same heaven. But beyond salvation there will be rewards for Christians according to their service, and Christians must give an account for their sins. Let no Christian think that he is getting by with his worldliness, his sin, his disobedience, his carelessness about soul-winning.

THE CHRISTIAN MUST MEET HIS DEEDS, GOOD AND BAD, AT CHRIST'S JUDGMENT SEAT

Read with me the shocking passage of Scripture in 2 Corinthians 5:9-10:

> Wherefore we labour, that, whether present or absent, we may be accepted of him. For we must all appear before the judgment seat of Christ; that every one may receive the things done in his body, according to that he hath done, whether it be good or bad.

Here we know why Paul worked so hard, why he endured such persecution, gave up home, family, good name, ease, honors, in order to win souls. He was laboring to be acceptable to Jesus Christ! He knew that he would one day meet the Saviour and longed to have Jesus say to him, "Well done, good and faithful servant" (Mt 25:23). Paul says, "For we must all appear before the judgment seat of Christ" (2 Co 5:10a). Do not confuse this with the final judgment of the unsaved as described in Revelation 20. Do not confuse this with the judgment of the Gentile world as described in Matthew 25: 31-46. Here is a judgment, in heaven, of Christians only. After we are already caught up to meet the Lord in the air, after we have resurrection bodies, after we see the Saviour, then "we must all appear before the judgment seat of Christ."

And what occurs at this judgment seat of Christ? "That every one may receive the things done in his body, according to that he hath done, whether it be good or bad" (2 Co 5:10b).

Do not explain away the plain statements of the Scriptures. The Christian is still to come face to face with his past. I know that the Christian has his sins forgiven as far as the destiny of his soul is concerned. It is true that all his sins are laid on Jesus and paid for on the cross. But God is still against sin. And up in heaven no Christian will think it did not matter that he sinned. Every Christian will find how horrible are the results of his sins. He will face what he has done, whether it be good or bad.

I do not wonder that, in the next verse, Paul says, "Knowing therefore the terror of the Lord, we persuade men" (2 Co 5:11). Paul knew that it would be a terrifying thing for Christians, born again, and even in glorified bodies, to stand up before Jesus Christ and give an account of the deeds done in the body both good and bad. In my sermon on "Tears in Heaven" in the book *And God Remembered*, I have discussed the tears of Christians when they face their sins in heaven. And I hope you will read it.

God may forgive sins, but there are some of the results of sin that will never be undone. In Evansville, Indiana, years ago, was a wicked, drunken sinner whom people called "Old Bill." He was a notorious bum. He often came to the Evansville Rescue Mission for help or for a bed. Sometimes he landed in jail drunk. Once he and an old crony got drunk together. In a drunken argument they fought and "Old Bill" got one eye put out.

Later "Old Bill" was wonderfully saved in the Evansville Rescue Mission. His life was transformed completely. He loved to tell what God had done for him. He went from church to church and gave a noble testimony of how he found Christ at the Evansville Rescue Mission, how God took away the taste for drink, and now he was respected and honored as a moral citizen, a greatly trusted Christian.

After he was saved he would introduce himself as "New Bill." He said that "Old Bill" was dead, that he was a new creature. It was not "Old Bill" any longer, but now it was "New Bill."

Yes, "Old Bill" was now "New Bill" and all the sins of the past were forgiven.

But how many eyes do you suppose "New Bill" had? "Old Bill" had an eye put out in a fight when he was a drunken sinner. Now that he was a born-again Christian he still had only one eye! God had forgiven the sin, but the man still had to live with the results of sin. So, even in heaven, a sinner who has been forgiven and who has peace with God must still meet the results of some of his sins.

FRUITLESS CHRISTIANS WILL "SUFFER LOSS" EVEN IN HEAVEN

At this judgment seat of Christ, when every Christian's works come to judgment, many Christians will see the deeds of a lifetime destroyed as worthless. This is discussed in 1 Corinthians 3:10-15:

> According to the grace of God which is given unto me, as a wise masterbuilder, I have laid the foundation, and another buildeth thereon. But let every man take heed how he buildeth thereupon. For other foundation can no man lay than that is laid, which is Jesus Christ. Now if any man build upon this foundation gold, silver, precious stones, wood, hay, stubble; every man's work shall be made manifest: for the day shall declare it, because it shall be revealed by fire; and the fire shall try every man's work of what sort it is. If any man's work abide which he hath built thereupon, he shall receive a reward. If any man's work shall be burned, he shall suffer loss: but he himself shall be saved; yet so as by fire.

The foundation is Jesus. No one need start to build a Christian life except after having Jesus Christ as his Saviour. But, having a new heart in

Christ, let every man take heed how he builds upon this foundation!

For up in heaven when Christians are judged before Jesus Christ, that building shall be revealed.

Some works of a Christian are like gold, silver, precious stones—building materials that do not burn, materials that last for ages. Some Christians' deeds are like building materials that will burn—wood, hay, stubble. At the judgment seat of Christ the fire of God's judgment will try every man's work of what sort it is. And verses 14 and 15 tell us, "If any man's work abide which he hath built thereupon, he shall receive a reward. If any man's work shall be burned, he shall suffer loss: but he himself shall be saved; yet so as by fire."

Read those verses again. You see that the Christian is still saved. He is saved, "yet so as by fire." His works are destroyed. Even up in heaven such a Christian will "suffer loss." And surely Christians will weep in heaven to see that they never did anything for which they could receive a reward.

Do not confuse salvation and rewards. Salvation is free. Those who trust in Jesus Christ and are born again already have salvation. But those whose works please Christ will receive a reward for them when they face the dear Saviour in heaven.

But many, many Christians will see how useless their lives were. Not a soul did they win to meet them in heaven! Not a thing did they do to bring glory to Christ though the endless ages! Such people will suffer loss at the judgment seat of Christ in heaven.

In 1 Corinthians 3:14 the man whose work will abide in heaven is promised, "He shall receive a reward." What kind of reward will God give to saints who serve Him devotedly here on earth?

Well, first, Christians who have been overcomers in this world will reign with Christ in the next world. The aged apostle Paul, shortly before his home-going, wrote to young Timothy, "It is a faithful saying: For if we be dead with him, we shall also live with him: if we suffer, we shall also reign with him: if we deny him, he also will deny us" (2 Ti 2:11-12).

Here Paul speaks of a blessed reward that will come to the faithful Christians, the faithful preacher. If we are willing to count ourselves dead here, we will live with Him there. If we suffer here for Jesus, we will reign also with Him. But if here we deny Him, then there He will deny us so far as open recognition is concerned. Part of the blessed reward is that we will reign with Christ.

To the church of Thyatira, the Lord Jesus sent this stirring message by the apostle John, "And he that overcometh, and keepeth my works unto the end, to him will I give power over the nations: and he shall rule them with a rod of iron; as the vessels of a potter shall they be broken to shivers: even as I received of my Father" (Rev 2:26-27).

Here the Lord has promised that when Jesus comes back to reign on the earth and sets up His Kingdom centered on the throne of David at Jerusalem that faithful Christians will help Him in a literal reign on earth!

Is not this the meaning also of the promise to overcoming individuals in Revelation 3:21? "To him that overcometh will I grant to sit with me in my throne, even as I also overcame, and am set down with my Father in his throne." Now Jesus is seated with the Father on His heavenly throne. One of these days when Jesus comes, clothed in garments of white, riding a white horse, with a great sword going forth from His mouth, to judge the nations of the earth and to reign on this earth which is His right, then faithful Christians will be seated with the Lord Jesus to reign, even as the dear Lord Jesus is now seated at the right hand of the Father!

Peter once wondered how all the poverty and sacrifice that the apostles went through could be repaid. He said, "Behold, we have forsaken all, and followed thee; what shall we have therefore?" (Mt 19:27).

Here is the answer Jesus gave: "Verily I say unto

67

you, That ye which have followed me, in the regeneration when the Son of man shall sit in the throne of his glory, ye also shall sit upon twelve thrones, judging the twelve tribes of Israel" (v. 28). Here is a clear promise that those who suffer and toil with Jesus here on earth will reign with Him hereafter.

That, too, seems to be much of the message of the parable of the pounds in Luke 19:11-27. To the man who had used his one pound diligently and gained more for his lord, the master said: "Well, thou good servant: because thou hast been faithful in a very little, have thou authority over ten cities" (v. 17). Then for the man who had cared for one pound for his Lord and had multiplied it to five, we have this word, "And he said likewise to him, Be thou also over five cities" (v. 19). I believe that the governors, senators, premiers, and judges in the millennial reign of Christ will be Christians who have been faithful in life here. Those who suffer with Him now will reign with Him then. And those who do well will be rewarded. Those who have sinned and failed will miss that reward.

THOSE WHO SIN MAY MISS THE ETERNAL FAME AND JOY OF THE SOUL-WINNER

The dearest thing to God's heart is to win souls. Winning souls is the first and main command for the Church, for the preacher, and for every Christian. The Great Commission is your commission and my commission. Jesus wants us to tell every creature and get people saved.

And God's greatest rewards are for the soul-winner. In Daniel 12:2-3, we read:

> And many of them that sleep in the dust of the earth shall awake, some to everlasting life, and some to shame and everlasting contempt. And they that be wise shall shine as the brightness of the firmament; and they that turn many to righteousness as the stars for ever and ever.

Oh, the eternal reward and praise and glory that will come to the soul winner! What joy to meet multitudes of sinners we have won to Christ! What joy to see the dear scarred face of the Saviour light up with joy over the multitudes we may have won to Christ with our earnest testimony, our sacrifice, our Spirit-filled pleading! Those who really win souls will have eternal joy over it in heaven.

Christians who go on in sin, who live worldly and fruitless lives, will miss the eternal joys of the soul-winner. How sad to miss all the righteous popularity, the glad public praises of Jesus Himself by not doing what He wants us to do, and especially by failing to win souls!

One of the blessings to which a Christian looks forward is that of seeing his loved ones again. Oh, how sweet it will be to see my mother who went to heaven when I was a boy hardly six years old! I could not look forward to heaven with much joy if I knew I would not meet my family there. My companion, my brothers and sisters will be there. I think no man ever had greater joy of his children than I have concerning my six lovely daughters. They are saved. They came to Christ very early and they are devoted Christians. But how sad I should be, even in heaven, if I should find my loved ones had gone to hell! To miss those that we love and should have won to Christ is part of the loss that some Christians must suffer in heaven.

Sin is a sad business. And even when we are in heaven, we will still be sad over our sins. Christians, beware of the terrible toll that disobedience and sinfulness and powerlessness will take when we meet at the judgment seat of Christ in heaven, and then in the ages beyond that.

Oh, how we should hate sin! It is said that when the emperor of Constantinople arrested Chrysostom and thought of trying to make him recant, the great preacher slowly shook his head. The emperor said to his attendants, "Put him in prison."

"No," said one of them, "he will be glad to go because he delights in the presence of his God in quiet."

"Well, then let us execute him," said the emperor.

"He will be glad to die," said the attendant, "for he wants to go to heaven. I heard him say so the

70

other day. There is only one thing that can give Chrysostom pain, and that is to make him sin; he said he was afraid of nothing but sin. If you make him sin you will make him unhappy."

Christians should fear sin like that and hate sin like that! God hates sin, and we must hate it too.

Let me say here that there is something abominable in any preaching that does not speak out against sin. It is compromise. It is tainted. It is unworthy of a preacher's vows and holy consecration. God hates sin and says so. Then let every true man of God hate sin and say so! Let every Christian learn to diligently root out sin as a poisonous, dangerous, and utterly hateful thing!

5

THE WAY TO FORGIVENESS
AND CLEANSING

WHEN A CHRISTIAN FALLS INTO SIN, for him it may
seem to be the end of the world. Peter had thrice
denied the Saviour. When the cock crowed that sad
morning Jesus was condemned to death, Peter went
out and wept bitterly. He gave up all thought of
the ministry and went back to the fishing business.
I can well understand the despair that settled over
Peter's spirit. Fellowship with God was broken, the
joy all gone. He had no assurance that God would
ever use him again, that God would ever hear him
pray, that he had even the right to call himself a
Christian. I think Peter's mind was in a turmoil of
hate for himself and his sin, and despair over ever
regaining the joyful fellowship and usefulness which
had been his. I am not surprised at his tears. I do
not wonder that the Lord Jesus had to solemnly
challenge him three times to prove his love by coming back to feed God's sheep, and win the lost souls
so dear to God.

I suppose that Peter could not believe that he

could, in a moment, have complete forgiveness and cleansing, have restored all the fellowship with the Saviour. I have known Christians, after they had sinned, to fall into the blackest despair. Some men have maimed themselves in self-inflicted punishment of the member that was used in sin. Some have committed suicide. Countless thousands of Christians have been in the "Slough of Despond," so well described by John Bunyan in *Pilgrim's Progress.* Feeling so guilty, so far removed from God's presence, they have imagined they have committed the unpardonable sin and that they are cast away forever from God's face!

Oh, poor, guilty, sinning child of God, I have good news for you! It is true that sin is wicked and hateful. Sin is murderous; it is tragedy unspeakable. No one can ever put into words the danger, the harm, the wickedness of the step when a child of God falls into sin. But thanks be to God, the Saviour has made a way of immediate forgiveness and cleansing and peace! As a poor sinner who has found mercy from God, let me tell you about the way to immediate forgiveness and cleansing, the way to complete restoration of fellowship with God.

Confession, God's Simple Condition of Forgiveness and Cleansing

First John 1:9 is a precious verse which has led millions of Christians to joy after sorrow, to glorious morning after a dark night of broken fellowship, to singing after sinning had brought shame. Read that Scripture with me: "If we confess our sins, he is faithful and just to forgive us our sins, and to cleanse us from all unrighteousness."

There it is. Any Christian who honestly confesses his sin to God has it instantly forgiven and cleansed away!

The same thing is taught in Proverbs 28:13: "He that covereth his sins shall not prosper: but whoso confesseth and forsaketh them shall have mercy."

Confession, that is, honest confession which includes the forsaking of sin, brings mercy immediately! Praise the Lord!

In another important passage of Scripture, Paul tells the Corinthian Christians, "For this cause many are weak and sickly among you, and many sleep" (1 Co 11:30). That is, sickness and death had come because of their sins. In 1 Corinthians 11:31 we are told, "For if we would judge ourselves, we should not be judged." That is, if you honestly take sides against your sin, admit your sin to God, plead guilty of it, condemn it, lament it, then God does not have to judge you. "If we would judge ourselves, we should not be judged."

When a child comes running to his father and says, "Daddy, I did wrong! Come see what I did! Oh, it was wicked! I am so sorry, so sorry. Please forgive me!" the father then does not need to punish the child. The child has already forsaken his sin, hated his sin, judged his sin. In response to that kind of honest confession there is immediate forgiveness from God. So says the blessed Word of God.

Does that seem too easy? Does it appear that God is too easy on sin when He instantly forgives the Christian who honestly judges his own sin, forsakes it, hates it, and confesses it? No, God does not do wrong in thus instantly forgiving the sin that is confessed honestly from the heart. In fact, God could not be faithful, could not be honest and just, if He did not forgive the sin that we hate, that we judge, that we confess, that we forsake! "If we confess our sins, he is faithful and just to forgive us our sins, and to cleanse us from all unrighteousness." God's justice, God's faithfulness is involved, and God must forgive.

The Ground of Our Forgiveness

There are glorious Bible doctrines involved which are the ground upon which God forgives His child when sin is confessed and forsaken. Based upon these glorious truths there rests a holy obligation upon God. God must do certain things which He has promised to do and which He has obligated Himself to do. God must forgive sin that is confessed and forsaken. Here I mention the holy ground of that forgiveness.

First of all, there is the blood of Christ. We should never forget, and God Himself cannot forget, that all of our sins are paid for with the precious blood of Christ. Remember the promise:

> Forasmuch as ye know that ye were not redeemed with corruptible things, as silver and gold, from your vain conversation received by tradition from your fathers; but with the precious blood of Christ, as of a lamb without blemish and without spot (1 Pe 1:18-19).

Oh, I do not wonder that God speaks of the blood as the "precious blood of Christ, as of a lamb without blemish and without spot." I hope that when I get to heaven God will let me preach and will teach me how to preach acceptably and adequately on "the precious blood of Christ." I have often longed to preach upon it and felt so helpless, so powerless, to tell how precious, how beyond all the gold and silver and precious stones, beyond all the banks and railroads and mines and property in the world in preciousness is this blood of Jesus Christ which paid the vast, dark, black, eternal debt of sin! That blood was shed for me! My sins, thank God, are paid for—every one.

When Jesus died on the cross He cried out, "It is finished" (Jn 19:30). He meant that now every jot and tittle, every faintest dust of sin had been paid for me and for every sinner who would accept

Christ's wonderful, atoning death on the cross in his stead, as the purchase price of his redemption. Sin is paid for! *My* sin is paid for. *All* my sins are paid for! All the sins of the past, all the sins of the present, all the sins of the future are paid for in full. Jesus Christ died once, and by that one sacrifice He purchased redemption and forgiveness for all my sins. "But this man, after he had offered one sacrifice for sins for ever, sat down on the right hand of God," and, "For by one offering he hath perfected for ever them that are sanctified" (Heb 10:12, 14). One sacrifice of the precious blood of Jesus was so valuable in its purity, its holiness; it so perfectly met all God's holy requirements that it paid for all my sin and all the sins of the whole world in one offering.

Now I have accepted that sacrifice as mine and that Saviour as my Saviour. Jesus became my Substitute and I accepted Him as such and God has approved Him as such. Therefore, God would be unjust if He did not give me the forgiveness which He has purchased. If God should withhold from one of His dear, penitent children the forgiveness and cleansing which is promised on the merits of the atoning blood of Christ, God would be dishonest. So, "if we confess our sins, he is faithful and just to forgive us our sins, and to cleanse us from all unrighteousness."

I wonder if the blood of Jesus Christ is precious

to you today? I do not mean only that once you were saved by the blood. I mean that today the precious blood of Christ still cleanses every child of God who confesses his sin.

I quoted 1 John 1:9 for you. Now let us go above that and read verses 3 to 7 in the same chapter:

> That which we have seen and heard declare we unto you, that ye also may have fellowship with us: and truly our fellowship is with the Father, and with his Son Jesus Christ. And these things write we unto you, that your joy may be full. This then is the message which we have heard of him, and declare unto you, that God is light, and in him is no darkness at all. If we say that we have fellowship with him, and walk in darkness, we lie, and do not the truth: But if we walk in the light, as he is in the light, we have fellowship one with another, and the blood of Jesus Christ his Son cleanseth us from all sin.

We note from this passage that it discusses fellowship, the fellowship of a Christian "with the Father, and with his Son Jesus Christ." John here is writing to Christians about their fellowship with God. He is not speaking to lost people about how to be saved, but to Christians about how to have fellowship.

Note in verse 4 that John says, "And these things write we unto you, that your joy may be full." People may be Christians and not be full of joy. Christians are really born again, yet may lack the assurance, the fellowship, the cleansing, the daily forgiveness and renewal that they need. But here, John says, is the way to fullness of joy and fellowship.

God does not have fellowship with darkness. God cannot have fellowship with sin. Sin, even in God's own dear child, is a dirty thing which God hates. The Christian who still condones sin, still covers sin, and makes an excuse for sin, does not have fellowship with God while he walks in darkness. A Christian walking in darkness who says he has fellowship with God, lies and does not the truth, we are told.

Now consider verse 7: "But if we walk in the light, as he is in the light, we have fellowship one with another, and *the blood of Jesus Christ his Son cleanseth us from all sin.*"

It is important to see that the word "cleanseth" in 1 John 1:7, quoted above, is in the present tense. The blood of Jesus Christ cleanses me today as I walk in the light, confessing and forsaking known sin. The blood was shed for me long ago, God applied it to my credit, and my soul is saved forever. But today, again, I can have the blessed cleansing of the blood. Praise the Lord, the blood of Jesus is the ground upon which Christians can claim forgiveness and cleansing every day. What Jesus Christ has purchased for us we have a right to claim, and we should claim. God is faithful and just to give us the forgiveness and cleansing which are purchased and which are promised!

But let us go a little further in this blessed teaching of cleansing and forgiveness in 1 John. In 2:1-2, this truth is repeated:

> My little children, these things write I unto you, that ye sin not. And if any man sin, we have an advocate with the Father, Jesus Christ the righteous: and he is the propitiation for our sins: and not for ours only, but also for the sins of the whole world.

Oh, we should not sin! John writes to us pleading that we do not sin. But, thank God, we have an advocate with the Father, Jesus Christ the righteous, who is the propitiation for our sins.

That leads me to further ground of our forgiveness and our cleansing from sin. That is, *Christ's high-priestly intercession for us.*

Some Christians believe that after Jesus died for us, and after we trust Him for salvation, we are left "on our own," that we are left like orphans with no one to take our part. Some Christians suppose that after the wonderful initial blessing of salvation, we have all the struggling to do on our own merit. But, thank God, that is not true. We have an Intercessor, a Mediator, a Peacemaker to intercede between us and God. "And if any man sin, we have an advocate with the Father, Jesus Christ the righteous."

It is a blessed promise that is given to us in Hebrews 7:24-27:

> But this man, because he continueth ever, hath an unchangeable priesthood. Wherefore he is able also to save them to the uttermost that come unto God by him, seeing he ever liveth to make intercession for them. For such an high priest became us, who is holy, harmless, undefiled, separate from sinners, and made higher than the heavens; who needeth not daily, as those high priests, to offer up sacrifice, first for his own sins, and then for the people's: for this he did once, when he offered up himself.

Jesus has an unchangeable priesthood. He ever lives to make intercession for us. He is "holy, harmless, undefiled." He offered one sacrifice, even Himself, and paid for sin. "Wherefore he is able also to save them to the uttermost that come unto God by him, seeing he ever liveth to make intercession for them." Those who are saved by the blood are saved "to the uttermost," because what Jesus began in His death on the cross, He day by day carries on, interceding for us at the right hand of God!

This is the right kind of High Priest for poor sinners such as we are, for He is a man who was tempted in all points like as we are and yet without sin.

Seeing then that we have a great high priest,

that is passed into the heavens, Jesus the Son of God, let us hold fast our profession. For we have not an high priest which cannot be touched with the feeling of our infirmities; but was in all points tempted like as we are, yet without sin. Let us therefore come boldly unto the throne of grace, that we may obtain mercy, and find grace to help in time of need (Heb 4:14-16).

Oh, we need not give up our profession because we have slipped into some kind of sin. Our High Priest knows our frailty and infirmity. His heart is touched. So let us not cast away our confidence, let us not despair, but rather, "let us therefore come boldly unto the throne of grace, that we may obtain mercy, and find grace to help in time of need."

It is not justice we need, but grace. It is not the rewards that we need, but mercy. Thank God, this is a throne of grace to which we come when we call on Jesus Christ! This dear High Priest, who was tempted in every way that any of us are ever tempted, asks us to be bold in our coming for mercy!

It is on grounds like these that God forgives the Christian who honestly confesses and judges his sin. It is because of facts like these that God can be faithful and can be just if He forgives the sin of the penitent Christian.

I would not leave the impression that Christ Jesus has a tender heart and that God the Father has a hard heart. I would not leave the impression that the dear Saviour is more willing to forgive us than is God the Father. No, the Father Himself gave His Son to pay our debt. Jesus loved, but it is also true that "God so loved the world" that He gave His Son to die for us.

The father heart of God is a tender heart. We could not believe and understand God's loving mercy until He could express that mercy in the person of His Son. Psalm 103 has a most gracious word for God's sinning children.

> The LORD is merciful and gracious, slow to anger, and plenteous in mercy. He will not always chide: neither will he keep his anger for ever. He hath not dealt with us after our sins; nor rewarded us according to our iniquities. For as the heaven is high above the earth, so great is his mercy toward them that fear him. As far as the east is from the west, so far hath he removed our transgressions from us. Like as a father pitieth his children, so the LORD pitieth them that fear him. For he knoweth our frame; he remembereth that we are dust (Ps 103:8-14).

God is not only holy; He is also merciful and gracious. He is slow to anger and plenteous in mercy. Praise the Lord, He will not always scold and nag about the Christian's sins that are confessed and forsaken. He will not keep His anger long. God does not set out to give us justice or deal with us on the merit of our sins when we honestly confess them and judge them. He gives us mercy instead of justice. What about the sin that is confessed and forsaken? "As far as the east is from the west, so far hath he removed our transgressions from us."

Do you think of Jesus as a High Priest who can be touched with the feeling of our infirmity? That is good, but Jesus, in that, is like the tender heart of His Father and our Father. "Like as a father pitieth his children, so the LORD pitieth them that fear him."

Sometimes when my children were small I was compelled to punish them for sin. A good sound whipping is painful to the child and more painful to the parent, but, oh, the blessed fruits of repentance that it brings! But I found that sometimes the work of repentance was already done. One of my six daughters was specially tenderhearted. Sometimes when some sin had caught up with her, she would come running to me with many, many tears, pleading for forgiveness. "I am so sorry, Daddy. Please forgive me! I'll never do it again!" Her tears and repentance did not wait for chastisement or scolding. How could I judge what she had already judged? How could I maintain wrath where she had already judged her sin? It is certainly hard to whip a child who is already penitent, who has already taken sides against his sin, who has sided in with the father for right.

Oh, God who knows our frame, who remembers that we are dust, and pities us with a father's pity for his children, has mercy, and the Father will quickly forgive the penitent child who confesses and turns from his sin!

Another ground of God's forgiveness, of any sin that is confessed, is the solid ground of God's promises in the Bible.

In the first place, God has promised everlasting life to His believing child.

> He that believeth on him is not condemned (Jn 3:18).

> He that believeth on the Son hath everlasting life (Jn 3:36).

> Verily, verily, I say unto you, He that heareth my word, and believeth on him that sent me, hath everlasting life, and shall not come into condemnation; but is passed from death unto life (Jn 5:24).

> My sheep hear my voice, and I know them, and they follow me: and I give unto them eternal life; and they shall never perish, neither shall any man pluck them out of my hand. My Father, which gave them me, is greater than all; and no man is able to pluck them out of my Father's hand (Jn 10:27-29).

God cannot damn His children. He has already

put within them the divine nature. He has already made in them a new man which cannot sin, "for his seed remaineth in him: and he cannot sin" (1 Jn 3: 9). God has already predestinated this child to be conformed to the image of His Son (Ro 8:29). Satan may have desired to sift you as wheat, but Jesus could say about every child of God who falls into sin, as He said to Peter, "I have prayed for thee, that thy faith fail not" (Lk 22:32). Now, an honest God must deal with His child on the basis of His fatherhood and His promise.

God must meet all the other promises of mercy. God must meet His own promise of Proverbs 28: 13 that "whoso confesseth and forsaketh them shall have mercy." He must meet His promise that "if we confess our sins, he is faithful and just to forgive us our sins, and to cleanse us from all unrighteousness." So, a faithful and just God has undertaken to take care of the sin question, not only for the past but for the future. God has obligated Himself to carry on the matter of our salvation until we awake in the likeness of His Son, Jesus! God has pledged Himself. Therefore, a faithful and just God must carry out His promises to His children.

A man buys a new automobile and has a three-month warranty. Within the period covered by that guarantee, the company is obligated to make good any defective part or workmanship. So, when God saves a soul, He not only furnishes the purchase price, but He guarantees the upkeep of salvation! A just and honest God, a faithful God who keeps His promises, must forgive His children when they come in penitence to confess and forsake sin!

Praise God for these holy grounds upon which a Christian can claim forgiveness!

WHAT CONFESSION INVOLVES

It is a blessed promise, that wonderful promise in 1 John 1:9. We can have the clear-cut assurance that "If we confess our sins, he is faithful and just to forgive us our sins, and to cleanse us from all unrighteousness." The very moment one confesses sin, and thus judges sin and takes sides with God against sin, that sin is blotted out, both forgiven and cleansed. Thus, upon simple confession of sin, the child of God has peace with God about the sin, and he has victory over the sin.

Of course, when God says confession, He means honest confession. So let every Christian solemnly consider what is involved in honest confession of sin.

FIRST, CONFESSION MEANS NOT ONLY THAT YOU ADMIT YOU DID THE THING, BUT YOU ADMIT THAT IT WAS A SIN.

Make sure that your wicked heart does not deceive you here. To say, "Lord, I did it, but I couldn't help myself; it was not really my fault" is not confession of sin but is excusing sin, taking sides with sin. If you want peace and forgiveness and cleansing, face sin honestly, call it by its right name, admit your guilt.

Many times Christian people say, "If I have done wrong, I want God to forgive me." That is no confession. As long as you put an *if* about your confession of sin, God puts an *if* about His forgiveness of that sin! I beg you, if you want mercy, face sin for the black thing it is, recognize it, admit it, take sides against it, judge it!

A woman came to D. L. Moody, it is said, to ask his help in a problem in her life. "I have a habit of exaggeration," she said. "Can you tell me how to overcome this bad habit of mine?"

Moody answered directly to the point. "Yes, the next time you are guilty of that sin, simply go to the person to whom you exaggerated and confess that you lied and that you are ashamed and sorry for it."

"Oh, but I wouldn't like to call it a lie!" said the woman.

"Yes," said Mr. Moody, "but if you do not call it a lie you will not quit it."

It is no honest confession that leaves the sin half covered, half excused, and still loved and defended.

Many a man has talked to me about a bad habit. I have found that the way to quit a bad habit is to face it honestly and call it a sin. As long as a man wants to quit tobacco and says he feels it is an unnecessary expense, and that perhaps it is bad for his health, he has not yet quit it. But when a man comes to say, "The use of tobacco for me is a sin; it defiles my body, the temple of the Holy Spirit; it wastes God's money, sets a bad example before my family and other young people; it is offensive to many and is a definite stumbling block to some, hinders my prayer life, hinders my soul-winning effort; it is a sin even to smoke one more cigarette; I ought to quit it to please Jesus Christ and to serve Him better," then a man can quit it. Do not trifle with sin, do not call it a nice name, do not look on it with allowance and with regard. Call it the sin that it is, hate it, turn from it in your heart.

SECOND, OF COURSE, ANY HONEST CONFESSION MEANS FORSAKING SIN.

For your mouth to say, "Lord, this is a sin, I am sorry," while the heart says, "But I still love it and I still plan to hold onto it," is no honest confession of sin. It is hypocrisy. Watch that deceitful heart of yours and make sure that it releases its grip on the sin that it pretends to confess. Sin that is not forsaken is not honestly confessed. Any straightforward confession of sin that will please God and gain His forgiveness and cleansing must involve the will. Does your will give up the sin? Do you want to be rid of it? Do you beg for cleansing? Does your mind cry out with brokenhearted David: "I acknowledge my transgressions: and my sin is ever before me. Create in me a clean heart, O God; and renew a right spirit within me. The sacrifices of God are a broken spirit: a broken and a contrite heart, O God, thou wilt not despise" (Ps 51:3, 10, 17)? The honest confession of sin ought to mean that you are sick of it, that you despise it, that you long to be cleansed from it. If you truly lament your sin and turn from it in your heart, judge it honestly: in the very moment of your confession, your sin will be forgiven and cleansed away and God will smile into your heart in sweet fellowship. Honest confession means honest repentance. "He that covereth his sins shall not prosper: but whoso confesseth and forsaketh them shall have mercy" (Pr 28:13).

THIRD, AN HONEST CONFESSION OF SIN, AN HONEST JUDGMENT OF SIN, WHEN YOU ASK FOR FORGIVENESS, OFTEN MEANS RESTITUTION.

In Miami, Florida, during my city-wide campaign with forty Baptist churches in about 1946, a pastor arose in a ministers' meeting and asked the chairman, "When I came to Christ and was saved, did not that mean that all my sins were under the blood, all forgiven?"

The chairman answered yes, that as far as one's salvation is concerned, all sins are under the blood the moment a sinner turns to Christ and trusts in Him.

"But what about debts I made when I was a drunken, unregenerate sinner?" asked the pastor.

"I believe that an honest man must still pay honest debts if he is to please God and have fellowship with God," replied the chairman.

The pastor began to weep and he said, "I think so, too. This morning I have paid two debts that I made in my wicked days without Christ. I have one more such debt to pay and then, thank God, there will be nothing between me and God!"

Oh, that pastor was right! Can any man honestly say that he is sorry for a debt unpaid, and still leave the debt unpaid? Can any Christian confess stealing, and hope to have the theft forgiven and cleansed, without restoring that which was stolen? Can one who has wronged a brother, and asked forgiveness of God, get the forgiveness and cleansing he craves without also trying to make right with the offended brother the sin he committed?

On this matter the Lord Jesus says, "Therefore if thou bring thy gift to the altar, and there rememberest that thy brother hath ought against thee; leave there thy gift before the altar, and go thy way; first be reconciled to thy brother, and then come and offer thy gift" (Mt 5:23-24).

One night in a Michigan city some years ago a woman was cut to the heart by my sermon on hindered prayer. She wrote me a note telling how eight years before she had stolen an expensive piece of jewelry, had pawned it, and spent the money. Now for years she had been prominent in church work. She dared not confess the sin, she said. It would bring public disgrace, possibly jail, certainly scandal. She wrote that she was tormented in conscience and begged me to tell her what to do.

"God has already told you what to do. I dare not tell you less," I wrote. After great struggle, after tossing sleeplessly till three o'clock in the morning, she said to Satan, "You old devil, for eight years you have ruined my peace and happiness! I will be done with this thing today. I have promised God that today I will go to the chief of police and confess the theft and ask him to help me make it right."

Then she went to sleep. When morning came she went to the chief of police, a Catholic man. Astonished, but deeply moved, he said, "Lady, you are a Protestant and I am a Catholic, but I will help anybody who wants to do right." So he sent a detective with her. They visited every pawnshop in town. To every pawnbroker she told the story of her sin and showed the pawn ticket.

But the watch was gone; she could not find it. There was only one thing left to do—go to the woman against whom she had sinned and confess the theft. When she wrote me about it, she said, "I expected her to scream at me, to accuse me, to call the police. I should not have been surprised had I gone to jail. Instead, she began to weep. She put her arms around me and said, 'Hush! we are sisters. We are Christians. Don't say another word. It is all forgiven, it is past.'

" 'But I will not hush. This has been on my heart for eight miserable years,' said the woman. 'I want you to say that you forgive me. I will pay you back with payments every payday beginning next Saturday.' "

The woman who had been wronged urged her friend to forget the matter and insisted that she wanted no payment. But now the good woman with holy zeal set out to pay her debt and honestly make restitution for the sin that she had long tried to confess, which she had tried to get cleansed away from her conscience without making restitution for the wrong done.

Now she wrote me, "I played the piano before, but I could not sing. I had no song in my heart. Now I sing all day! Better yet, when I pray, God smiles down in my face and it seems I can have anything I ask. Oh, it is wonderful to have nothing between God and me and have peace with Him again!"

Dear, troubled soul, if you have sinned against somebody else, go make it right! Any honest confession of sin means that you will judge it, do all you can do to undo it.

The famous evangelist, Gipsy Smith, in his sermon, "Slay Utterly," tells of a striking case. Let us tell it in Gipsy Smith's own words:

At the close of an inquiry meeting the wife of one of the ministers came to see me. She said, "There is a young lady who wants to speak to you; she refuses to go away. Nobody seems to be able to help her; she will speak to the preacher."

I said, "I will go with you," and we went into the room. I went to the other end of the room and spoke to this poor person.

She said, "Sir, I want to confess an awful sin. I am a mother, and I fathered my child on an innocent man. He was a student in one of the theological colleges studying for the ministry, and I blighted his life as well as branded him. I took him through three courts and won my case, but I have a bit of Hell inside. He was dismissed and disgraced, and he is as innocent as you are. What am I to do?"

"Do?" I said; "do right."

She said, "I have no peace."

"And you never will have peace," I said. "In this world you may have pardon on condition, but there is no such thing as peace for you, for you will never forgive yourself that wrong." I could not spare her. I had to be faithful in order to save her. I said—

"You must take off that brand as publicly as you put it on—just as publicly."

"Oh, sir!" she said, "he will send me to prison."

I said, "If it means prison, and you go to prison, you will go with the consciousness that you made an honest attempt to undo the wrong, but for you the way to Heaven is *via* that confession, and there is no such thing as joy or peace in God for you without taking up your cross."

I shall never forget the effect my words made on that poor person. She bent, she collapsed, and my heart ached for her. Yet I dared not heal the hurt of that poor person slightly, nor cry "Peace" falsely. I had to be faithful, and as I knelt beside her, I said—

"When you are willing as far as lies in your power to undo the wrong, God will help you, and He will not forsake you."

Presently she bit her lip till it bled, and, clasping the chair in front of her, she said, "O God, I will do it if it means prison."

It was not an easy path for that poor person, but she walked it bravely. She went back to the court—and I am speaking of what was in all the London papers—she went back to the court, and had the court revise the whole case, and in that crowded court she said, when they asked her why she made this confession, "Because I gave my heart to God, and I had to take this course to clear my conscience of its guilt."

Her confession relieved her own heart of its burden, cleared an innocent man, and made an impression on that city which is felt today. The only path of peace is the path of righteousness.

Slay utterly, put away the evil thing, obey God. Put Him in His right place, and the joy and peace will come.

Yes, it is true, blessedly true, "If we confess our sins, he is faithful and just to forgive us our sins, and to cleanse us from all unrighteousness," even as the Scripture promises. Just make sure it is honest confession, a confession that judges the sin honestly, that repents of the sin and turns from it, and that does anything that properly can be done to undo the sin. Anything less than that is not an honest confession of sin. Do not fail to have the forgiveness and cleansing that you need by dealing lightly or dishonestly with sin.

NOW, BELIEVE GOD, ACCEPT AND REJOICE IN THE FORGIVENESS THAT HE FREELY GIVES.

Have you confessed your sin to God? Have you turned away from it? Have you done all you can do to stop the evil effect of the sin? Then I beg you, dear troubled soul, believe what God has said and take the forgiveness.

Often people write me, "Oh, pray for God to forgive me! I committed a terrible sin. I weep and pray, but I cannot have forgiveness." Such letters always grieve me greatly. I always answer honestly, saying that what they need is not more prayer, but simply to believe God. Oh, how you dishonor God, how you grieve His tender heart, and how you misjudge His mercy when you will not believe that He forgives when He says He forgives. Here is one place that to take God at His Word is vital. Why should one who has sinned and failed God, now continually torment himself after he has turned his heart away from the sin? Nothing you could do would honor God more than to thank Him for forgiveness, believe it and rejoice in it, and cast out all the bitter memories of the sin and the estrangement from God which followed.

When I was in a revival campaign in Clarksburg, West Virginia, a man brought his wife all the way from Alabama to talk with me. She felt that she had sinned, that God would not forgive her, that she had committed some sin that was unpardonable. I told her that she was only one of hundreds with whom I had dealt on the same matter. I told her what I now tell you: No Christian can commit the unpardonable sin. Thank God, all our sins are already paid for. Every sin, every failure, every offense, every transgression was paid for on the cross by the blood of Jesus Christ. For every one of them He has interceded at the throne of grace. Now God deals with you not as an alien, not as a lost sinner, not as a condemned criminal against God; God deals with you now as a beloved child, erring and weak, but so dear to His tender heart! God wants you to take freely the forgiveness which He gives with such love. Read that Scripture again, believe it, take God up on it today, and begin to live in the perfect peace of knowing that sin is forgiven and blotted out! "If we confess our sins, he is faithful and just to forgive us our sins, and to cleanse us from all unrighteousness."

In Dallas, Texas, I held revival services in a big rented furniture building while our brick tabernacle was under construction. One night a woman with a sad face, with many of the marks of sin, sat before me. She wept as I preached, and silently wiped the tears away. When I gave an invitation for sinners to come to Christ, she wept all the more but would not come. I stepped down to her side and whispered, urging her to come to Christ. She said, "No, I cannot! I wish I could, but I cannot!"

When I insisted, she said, "Preacher, please don't torment me. There is nothing I can do about it. I cannot come."

When I asked why she could not come, she said, "Oh, because I cannot forget what I have done! I can never forget what I have done!"

God led me to turn to a Scripture which is dear to my heart, as it ought to be to every erring and frail sinner: "This is the covenant that I will make with them after those days, saith the Lord, I will put my laws into their hearts and in their minds will I write them; and their sins and iniquities will I remember no more" (Heb 10:16-17).

I showed her that if she would trust Jesus, all the

98

past would be forgiven and blotted out, and God would put it in her heart to serve Him. God would even forget that she had sinned. God would never even bring the sins to mind again! Then I said to her, "If God is so willing to forgive and forget, and will never remember these sins against you any-more, can't you forget them, too?"

I remember how the tears rained down her face. I remember the gladness with which she saw that God would not only save her from her sin, but would take away all the bitter memories, take away the eternal condemnation in her own heart; that He would forget and would help her to forget! So she came gladly to trust such a Saviour. Now, I assure you that every poor sinner who hates his sins can come immediately for salvation and have it. Every erring Christian who honestly confesses his sins, turns from them, and judges them in his heart, can, in a moment, be assured that God has blotted them out and that He will remember them no more against him! Oh, blessed promise!

I do not wonder that some sinning saint has wept all through the night over sins. So have I. God knows my repentance has been deeper and more bit-ter since I have been saved than it was when I came to Christ as a nine-year-old boy. David said, "My tears have been my meat day and night" (Ps 42:3). He pleaded with God, "A broken and a contrite heart, O God, thou wilt not despise" (51:17). But, do you think that God wants you to continue in sorrow and self-reproaches? Do you think God wants you to continue in morbid self-accusation after you have honestly faced your sin, confessed it, forsaken it? No, no! God wants you to claim the forgiveness He has offered, believe Him, and be happy.

It is needless to look back and weep over the sins you have honestly confessed and forsaken. It is needless to look forward in fear as to whether you will fall short in the future. You are weak enough, God knows, but His grace is sufficient.

Annie Johnson Flint, in the poem "But We See Jesus," has a sweet and comforting word here.

I don't look back, God knows the fruitless efforts,
    The wasted hours, the sinning, the regrets,
I leave them all with Him who blots the record,
    And mercifully forgives, and then forgets.

I don't look forward, God sees all the future,
    The road that, short or long, will lead me home,
And He will face with me its every trial,
    And bear for me the burdens that may come.

But I look up—into the face of Jesus,
    For there my heart can rest, my fears are stilled,
And there is joy, and love, and light for darkness,
    And perfect peace, and every hope fulfilled.*

Do you, dear Christian, take the forgiveness God

*© Evangelical Publishers, Toronto, Canada. Reproduced by permission.

promised? I trust you will set out to make this a daily matter, every day confessing any known sin that has come up to mar your fellowship with God, every day instantly claiming forgiveness for it when you judge it and forsake it. That way you can live the happy, joyful life of fellowship.

6

LIVING A LIFE OF VICTORY OVER SIN

WE HAVE DISCUSSED the blessed promise that a Christian may confess his sin, judge his sin, and be instantly forgiven and cleansed. But, must a Christian have an up-and-down experience? Thank God, no! A Christian can live on a high plane of victory over sin and have peace with God. He can walk in the daily light of God's presence and have sweet, constant fellowship with God, led and comforted by the Spirit and used in soul-winning.

EVERY CHRISTIAN MAY LIVE VICTORIOUSLY EVERY DAY

A Negro spiritual plaintively expresses the experience of too many Christians:

> I'm sometimes up and I'm sometimes down,
> Comin' for to carry me home.

A song I remember from my childhood says:

> Once I thought I walked with Jesus,
> Yet such changeful moods I had;

Sometimes trusting, sometimes doubting,
  Sometimes joyful, sometimes sad.

But He drew me closer to Him,
  Bade my doubting, fearing cease,
And when I had fully yielded,
  Filled my soul with perfect peace!

Now I'm trusting every moment,
  Nothing less could be enough.
And my Saviour bears me gently
  O'er those places once so rough.

Oh, what peace my Saviour gives,
  Peace I never knew before.
And my way has brighter grown
  Since I learned to trust Him more.

F. A. BLACKMER

It is a blessed truth that a Christian can live in daily content, daily peace, daily victory.

CHRIST HAS PURCHASED DAILY, COMPLETE VICTORY FOR EVERYONE WHO TRUSTS HIM.

Dear child of God, do you know where you are headed? You are headed for the resurrection and will awake conformed to the image of God's dear Son! (Ro 8:29). David knew this and said, "I shall be satisfied, when I awake, with thy likeness" (Ps 17:15).

Paul the apostle knew the blessed victory that one can have through the price paid on Calvary and through the help of a risen Saviour. He said:

103

But what things were gain to me, those I counted loss for Christ. Yea doubtless, and I count all things but loss for the excellency of the knowledge of Christ Jesus my Lord: for whom I have suffered the loss of all things, and do count them but dung, that I may win Christ, and be found in him, not having mine own righteousness, which is of the law, but that which is through the faith of Christ, the righteousness which is of God by faith: That I may know him, and the power of his resurrection, and the fellowship of his sufferings, being made conformable unto his death; if by any means I might attain unto the resurrection of the dead. Not as though I had already attained, either were already perfect: but I follow after, if that I may apprehend that for which also I am apprehended of Christ Jesus. Brethren, I count not myself to have apprehended: but this one thing I do, forgetting those things which are behind, and reaching forth unto those things which are before, I press toward the mark for the prize of the high calling of God in Christ Jesus (Phil 3:7-14).

It is true that this life of victory cost Paul much. All the things that were gain, Paul counted loss for Christ. He gave them up and did not depend upon them. For Jesus Christ, he suffered the loss of all things and said, I "do count them but dung." So, he found, not his own righteousness, but the righteousness of Christ and gave up everything in order to know Him "and the power of his resurrection, and the fellowship of his sufferings, being made conformable unto his death." Paul really tried to live as if he were raised from the dead.

Paul knew that he had not attained the resurrection, neither was he perfect. But Paul followed after, running after the glorious resurrected life that one day all of us will have. Paul forgot the things that were behind and reached after the things before, the glorious resurrection and the perfection that will be ours when we awake transformed in the likeness of Christ. Paul did not claim to be "wholly sanctified" in the sense of sinless perfection, nor to have perfect love. Paul did not claim to have apprehended, and he plainly denied that he was already perfect. But what victory and joy and peace Paul had in daily life!

Writing to the saints at Rome, by divine inspiration Paul commanded as follows:

Likewise reckon ye also yourselves to be dead indeed unto sin, but alive unto God through Jesus Christ our Lord. Let not sin therefore reign in your mortal body, that ye should obey it in the lusts thereof. Neither yield ye your members as instruments of unrighteousness unto sin: but yield yourselves unto God, as those that are alive from the dead, and your members as instruments of righteousness unto God. For sin shall not have dominion over you: for ye are not under the law, but under grace (Ro 6:11-14).

Every Christian is to reckon himself dead to sin. Every Christian is to determine that sin shall not reign in his mortal body. We must confess that we still have the old nature. We have the frail body and the frail fleshly nature that goes with the body, and will have until death or until Jesus comes to change our vile bodies. That body and fleshly nature will then be adopted and redeemed, as we learn in Romans 8:19-23. But, while we have the old body and the old nature, it need not reign. It can be mortified, kept under. It can be ruled by the victorious and spiritual Christian.

Every Chrisian who, upon his profession of faith, has been baptized into the likeness of Christ's death and has been raised in the likeness of His resurrection, in his baptism professed faith that Christ is risen from the dead, and that one day we, too, shall rise from the dead. When Jesus died, He died in my place. When He rose from the dead, then He pictured that I, too, will rise from the dead. So I count myself dead to sin and alive to Christ, and I set out to live a life in the power of the resurrected Christ. Every Christian can and should so live.

GOD'S GRACE, FREELY AVAILABLE, IS SUFFICIENT FOR EVERY NEED OF THE CHRISTIAN.

I shall never forget when I first learned that God's

grace is sufficient under all circumstances, any time when defeat threatens and when strength fails, when discouragement comes, when temptation is great. I had been called to the First Baptist Church of Shamrock, Texas, my first full-time pastorate. The little church was divided, defeated, worldly. It had been without a pastor for long months. Lightning had struck the church building and burned it down. The people worshiped in a little unpainted, board tabernacle, forty by sixty feet. I felt clearly led to accept the pastorate and did; then I began revival services in the church. Because of quarrels and division, many had vowed they would never enter that church again. For a week the heavens wept and rain drowned out the services. Only a handful of the faithful appeared. Deeply burdened and troubled, I went alone among the rocks in a railroad cut and searched in my Bible until I found the blessed promises of 2 Corinthians 12. Paul had been greatly exalted, had been given great blessings. Then there came trouble and trial, weakness, temptation.

> And lest I should be exalted above measure through the abundance of the revelations, there was given to me a thorn in the flesh, the messenger of Satan to buffet me, lest I should be exalted above measure. For this thing I besought the Lord thrice, that it might depart from me. And he said unto me, My grace is sufficient for thee:

for my strength is made perfect in weakness. Most gladly therefore will I rather glory in my infirmities, that the power of Christ may rest upon me. Therefore I take pleasure in infirmities, in reproaches, in necessities, in persecutions, in distresses for Christ's sake: for when I am weak, then am I strong (2 Co 12:7-10).

I read those verses, read them again and again, and wept before the Lord. I admitted my frailty, my weakness, my youth, my inexperience. Then I claimed the blessed promise that God's grace would be sufficient, that God's strength is made perfect in weakness. Like Paul, I began to say, "Most gladly therefore will I rather glory in my infirmities, that the power of Christ may rest upon me. Therefore I take pleasure in infirmities, in reproaches, in necessities, in persecutions, in distresses for Christ's sake: for when I am weak, then am I strong."

Thank God, all the reproaches, all the infirmities of the flesh and spirit, all the necessities and poverty, all the persecutions, all the trials, are nothing but trifles for the abundant grace of God! God can do anything but fail. *Man's extremity is God's opportunity*. Man's infirmity simply makes an open door for God's blessing if the man but trusts Him. Oh, the abundant, amazing grace of God! That grace, freely available day and night for the Christian, is always sufficient.

The grace of God in forgiving, in giving a new

chance, in giving strength for weakness, in overcoming the circumstances, is such a basic strength that every Christian may live in constant victory. Praise the Lord for the grace of God!

GOD GIVES DAILY LIGHT FOR OUR DAILY WALK.

In this matter of daily fellowship, daily cleansing, daily joy, daily light, we have blessed promises. In 1 John 1:3-7 we are given these comforting words:

> That which we have seen and heard declare we unto you, that ye also may have fellowship with us: and truly our fellowship is with the Father, and with his Son Jesus Christ. And these things write we unto you, that your joy may be full. This then is the message which we have heard of him, and declare unto you, that God is light, and in him is no darkness at all. If we say that we have fellowship with him, and walk in darkness, we lie, and do not the truth: but if we walk in the light, as he is in the light, we have fellowship one with another, and the blood of Jesus Christ his Son cleanseh us from all sin.

This passage is given to teach a Christian to have daily fellowship with the Father and with His Son Jesus Christ. John says, "And these things write we unto you, that your joy may be full." Oh, the daily, abundant, overflowing joy which a Christian may have, promised in these verses!

It is true that if we walk in darkness, fellowship

will be broken. But, "if we walk in the light, as he is in the light, we have fellowship one with another, and the blood of Jesus Christ his Son cleanseth us from all sin."

We learn here a blessed lesson. A Christian can have daily light on his path. He can know ahead of time and avoid the stones and pitfalls in the road. A Christian is not left alone, compelled to stumble in ignorance and weakness in a wicked world, attacked by Satan, and misled by his own carnal nature. No, a Christian can be led by the nail-pierced hands of Jesus, can walk on the pathway with daily light and with constant fellowship and joy.

One source of light to the Christian is the Bible, the blessed Word of God. The Administrator of this light is the Holy Spirit. A Christian can have the Spirit of God to guide him as he studies the Bible, to bring to his mind the warnings, the promises, the comforts. A Christian can have the solemn rebuke of the Holy Spirit for failure and sin, and the sweet comfort of the Holy Paraclete, the Comforter, who is sent alongside to help and to guide us into all truth.

In view of all these blessed promises, let the Christian enter into the life of peace and victory. Remember Jesus said, "Let not your heart be troubled: ye believe in God, believe also in me" (Jn 14: 1). Again He said, "Peace I leave with you, my peace I give unto you: not as the world giveth, give

I unto you. Let not your heart be troubled, neither let it be afraid" (Jn 14:27).

Now let us learn how to walk in the light.

How to Live Victoriously Every Day

Let me give some simple rules which are, if followed sincerely and from the heart, the certain road to daily victory—victory over sin, victory over defeat, victory over discouragement and every trial and trap set by Satan.

CONFESS BEFORE GOD AND JUDGE EVERY SIN THE MOMENT IT BECOMES KNOWN TO YOU.

Keep short accounts with God! Do not wait until you have backslidden, have lost your joy, and have fallen into worldliness and open and coarser sins. Make it a rule of your life that the moment God shows you failure or sin in your life, that you will confess and forsake it. Thank God, a small matter is soon mended. If everything else in the kitchen is spotlessly clean and in its place, the dishes of one meal can soon be washed and put away. But if Mother has been gone from home for a week and the sink is filled with dirty dishes, every pot and pan is encrusted with burned food, the garbage pail is running over, it is a discouraging task to put things right. The moment a sin is recognized, confess and forsake it. That one rule is the biggest rule, and it works. "For if we would judge ourselves, we should not be judged" (1 Co 11:31).

DAILY MEDITATION AND FEEDING ON THE WORD OF GOD GIVE LIGHT AND STRENGTH FOR VICTORY.

Two verses in Psalm 119 tell us how valuable the Word of God is in overcoming sin. Verse 9 says, "Wherewithal shall a young man cleanse his way? By taking heed thereto according to thy word."

Every young man who sets out, day by day, to find from the Word of God, God's rules of conduct and blessed truths as applied to his life, can "cleanse his way."

Verse 11 in the same psalm says, "Thy word have I hid in mine heart, that I might not sin against thee."

Here we see that it is important for a Christian to memorize Scriptures, to learn what God says and meditate on it in the heart. Then the Word of God, hidden in the heart, comes to the conscience in time of stress and temptation and reminds one, "Don't do that! That is a sin."

When some great temptation comes, it is too late to search for God's warning. Hide it in the heart ahead of time if you would have help when you need it to keep your heart from sin.

A few years ago several of us, as guests of a Christian sportsmen's group, went to the Rocky Mountains to hunt. We wanted a grizzly bear. So we bought an outlaw horse for $25 and used him as a pack horse (with many tribulations because of his rebellion) to pack camp goods up into the high Rockies, just east of Yellowstone Park. The outlaw horse was then shot and used as bait for Mr. Grizzly Bear. Many times we went to visit the bear bait to see if Mr. Grizzly had come to eat his fill of the decaying carcass. I assure you that every time we came with the 30-30 rifle loaded and cocked. Should we come face to face with a giant grizzly as big as a horse, the most murderous beast on this continent, it would be too late to load the gun.

Oh, Christian, keep your gun loaded! Then when you meet the devil going about as a roaring lion seeking whom he may devour, you can defend yourself against him with the sword of the Spirit. Meditate on the Word of God, hide it in your heart, and you will be forewarned and forearmed against temptation.

In the high-priestly prayer of Jesus, the Saviour prayed for all of us, "Sanctify them through thy truth: thy word is truth" (Jn 17:17). A Christian can be set apart for God by the Word of God.

Paul gave the same holy injunction to the preachers at Ephesus. "I commend you to God, and to the word of his grace, which is able to build you up, and to give you an inheritance among all them which are sanctified" (Ac 20:32).

The really victorious life is the life that is

grounded on the Word of God, that feeds on the Word of God, that is cleansed by the blessed Word of God.

We are told in Ephesians 5:25-26 that "Christ also loved the church, and gave himself for it; that he might sanctify and cleanse it with the washing of water by the word." So, let every Christian read all of the Bible, read much of it every day, hide it in his heart, obey it, love it, meditate upon it day and night. That is an essential part of the sure road to daily victory.

AVOID THE FIRST STEPS THAT WOULD LEAD TO SIN.

We are told in 1 Thessalonians 5:22, "Abstain from all appearance of evil," or "abstain from every form of evil." I think the idea here is not only that we should keep the appearance of doing right but also make sure we shun the approach to evil. It is true that we ought to provide things honest in the sight of all men. But I think this Scripture means more than that. It means, surely, that a Christian should avoid the outlying area of sin, avoid the steps that would lead to sin.

A few weeks ago a mother, who was sending her brilliant young Christian son to a modernistic school, asked me to pray for her son. They wanted him to have the courses offered in this school where the verbal inspiration of the Bible is denied, where the virgin birth, the bodily resurrection, the atoning death of Christ are mocked. She wanted me to pray that her boy would stay true to the faith despite the certain temptation he was voluntarily entering. I told her I would pray for the boy but that I had no assurance that God would answer such a prayer after they deliberately subjected the young man to such temptation.

I know how to raise young people as sound Christians, well established in the faith, and able to resist all the foolish and wicked blandishments of modernism. But the only way I know to do that is to rear them right, without putting them into deliberate temptation in such matters. Then they will be strong and reliable and able to meet whatever comes in the course of duty. I do not believe that a Christian can always overcome a temptation when he has deliberately walked into the temptation.

David could have avoided the sin of adultery, but it is very possible that he could not have avoided it after he had brought Bathsheba to his rooftop in the night and dallied and petted with another man's wife. David could have avoided murdering his good friend and faithful servant, Uriah, but I do not know that he could have avoided it after he had committed adultery with the man's wife and felt compelled to hide it. Lot could have avoided incest with his daughters, but he could not avoid it after he was drunk and did not know what was going on.

Young men have told me of harowing temptation

and shameful defeat in sex temptation. I have told them, as I now tell you, that the place to have victory is before you read the dirty story, before you look at the lewd picture, before your mind dwells on forbidden topics, before you neck and pet and unduly stimulate sex desire and set the fires of hell burning in your own breast. Yes, a Christian can live a happy, victorious life, but he cannot do that and play with sin.

Children who do not want to start fires should not play with matches. The girl who does not want to fall in love with and marry a drunkard should make up her mind never to have a date with a boy who drinks, or with a boy or man unworthy to be her husband. You who do not want to follow the lewd practices of the movie stars and to have the shameful blight of daily defeat by sin, should not look on the silver screen with its tainted pictures, its false standards, its deceitful lusts. If you put yourself in the company of the wicked, immoral stars of Hollywood, you will soon be living as they live, and your heart will be shamed over your defeat.

In Joshua 7 is the story of the sin and ruin that came to Achan. He took a Babylonish garment and a wedge of gold of fifty shekels weight and 200 pieces of silver. The progress of sin is illustrated in his words, "When I saw among the spoils a goodly Babylonish garment, and two hundred shekels of silver, and a wedge of gold of fifty shekels weight, then I coveted them, and took them; and, behold, they are hid in the earth in the midst of my tent, and the silver under it" (Josh 7:21).

Note the deadly course of sin, "I saw . . . I coveted . . . and took . . . they are hid." First we look on sin. Then we want sin. Then we take sin. Then we excuse it, lie about it, hide it. I cannot promise any Christian that he will not take the forbidden things if he first looks on them, then grows to covet them. So let every Christian start out to avoid the very appearance of evil, to avoid the steps that will lead to sin. This is the road of victory.

SEEK TO FOLLOW THE BLESSED WILL OF GOD IN EVERY DETAIL.

This rule is akin to the one mentioned above. But the one who sets out to do the will of God in everything can have God's help in time of need.

Years ago in Dallas, Texas, a young man in the church of which I was pastor felt the call of God to preach. A business opportunity came his way, a good job, fast promotion, a good salary. He tried the newspaper business and seemed to prosper in it, but he did not prosper spiritually. Preoccupation with his work, missing church services, neglect of Bible study and prayer, a heart growing cold toward soul-winning followed, and then, finally, drink and the consciousness that he had drifted far from the will of God and the blessing of God.

I remember when he came forward in a public service to lay down his life again upon the altar. With many tears he said to me, "Brother Rice, I cannot even be a good Christian if I do not preach the Gospel as God has commanded me!"

He had learned the hard lesson that if you do not obey the will of God you cannot have God's strength, God's victory, and God's help in overcoming temptation.

I know that the dear Lord has a way whereby the man who has been a slave to drink can be utterly freed from it and live a victorious life, with never again a touch of liquor, but a life of sobriety and holy example for others, a life of sweet fellowship and rich usefulness. I have seen many a drunkard saved and transformed, and I have seen the victory that God has given over such temptations. But I say frankly—as I have found it necessary to tell many a drinking man—that I cannot guarantee victory over drink if he holds onto cigarettes. I cannot guarantee that God will give victory over the lust for liquor if he still makes money his god, if he does not take time for the Bible, time to pray, and does not have a heart to win souls. The only way wherein lies full and complete victory day by day is the life of obedience to the will of God.

That is the reason it is so desperately important

for every Christian to listen to the still small voice, the monitoring of the Holy Spirit within. The blessed Holy Spirit is sent to comfort, to guide, to warn the believer. Thank God, this holy Comforter and Guide lives within our bodies. He helps us pray; He helps us live victoriously. But the Scripture plainly commands not only "Walk in the Spirit" (Gal 5:16) and "Be filled with the Spirit" (Eph 5:18) , but "grieve not the holy Spirit of God" (Eph 4:30) and "Quench not the Spirit" (1 Th 5:19) .

The Christian who wants to live a victorious life must listen to the still small voice. Do not quench the insistent warning when God's Spirit speaks to the heart about sin. If today you defend your actions, if you do not follow the light and walk in the light, then the light may be withdrawn. God's Spirit may cease to warn.

As we are not to quench the Spirit by rebellion, so we are not to grieve the Spirit by sin. Everything that grieves the blessed Holy Spirit who lives within us should be hated and lamented and judged. The ungrieved Spirit will give us joy and peace and victory. Let us make sure that that holy Guest within us is not grieved by any tolerance of sin, by any rebellion against the will of God, by any disobedience to the heavenly vision.

GOD GIVES STRENGTH IN ANSWER TO CEASELESS PRAYER.

In the model prayer the Saviour taught us to pray, "Lead us not into temptation, but deliver us from evil" (Mt 6:13). So it is obviously intended that we should daily pray for guidance, pray for deliverance from the evil one. In Ephesians 6:10-17, we are commanded to be strong in the Lord, and in the power of His might; to put on the whole armor of God, with loins girt about with truth, with the breastplate of righteousness, with shoes of the Gospel of peace, the shield of faith, the helmet of salvation, and the sword of the Spirit. Then verse 18 continues, "Praying always with all prayer and supplication in the Spirit, and watching thereunto with all perseverance and supplication for all saints."

The final equipment of the good soldier, who wrestles against principalities and powers and defends himself by God's help against all the onslaughts of the evil one is prayer. The Christian should pray always, with all prayer and supplication in the Spirit and with all perseverance for all the saints. What a weapon is prayer!

A Christian man came to me, his pastor, for help in breaking the tobacco habit which had enslaved him for many years. He agreed with me that it was a sin to defile the body, that it was a bad example before his children and others, that it dishonored Christ and was a poor testimony for a Christian. He wanted to quit but thought he could not. I prevailed upon him to trust the Lord and try. He came back to report to me. "If I could only talk to you several times a day and have your advice and have you pray for me, I could win this fight," he said. "I go out in the morning after we have our family worship and I feel strong. I get along well. After two or three hours I become so obsessed with a desire for a smoke that I can hardly control myself. Thus far I have not been able to get through the day without smoking. What shall I do?"

I told him, as I tell you today, dear troubled Christian, that you may have strength for every need by constant prayer. Anyone who follows the will of God and who really wants to do right can have grace to do right. But it is only by constant prayer that one may have such strength. I urged upon this troubled Christian that he take time to pray in the morning, then simply go aside once every hour, as long as necessary, to confess his weakness, to plead with God for strength, to wait on God until he had sweet assurance of God's help.

He tried that plan and found himself wonderfully, happily victorious. He said, "I promise God that I will pray every half hour if need be, or every fifteen minutes, just so He will help me to gain the victory in this matter." Soon the fight was won, the filthy habit was broken, and the Christian man, who had a Christian heart, had also a good Christian testimony.

Simon Peter missed the point of the solemn warning Jesus gave him and fell into sin. The Lord Jesus said, "Watch and pray, that ye enter not into temptation: the spirit indeed is willing, but the flesh is weak" (Mt 26:41). If Peter had watched and prayed as he should have, his weak flesh would not have led him into lying, denying Jesus and cursing and swearing. The right kind of continual waiting on God in prayer would have given Peter the strength to do right.

God is a strong tower of refuge for those who run to Him regularly, in every need, in every temptation.

This way of perfect peace and victory through taking everything to God in prayer is taught in Philippians 4:6-7, "Be careful for nothing; but in every thing by prayer and supplication with thanksgiving let your requests be made known unto God. And the peace of God, which passeth all understanding, shall keep your hearts and minds through Christ Jesus." God's peace, like a strong garrison of soldiers, keeps and defends the heart and keeps it in perfect fellowship and victory if we take every burden, every trouble, every temptation to God in prayer with supplication and thanksgiving. So then, dear Christian, learn to "pray without ceasing" (1 Th 5:17).

> Have we trials and temptations?
> Is there trouble anywhere?

. . . .

122

Jesus knows our ev'ry weakness,
Take it to the Lord in prayer.

J. SCRIVEN

FERVENT SOUL-WINNING EFFORT HELPS TO KEEP
ONE STRAIGHT, BRINGS GOD'S BLESSING IN FELLOWSHIP.

All we have said before about living a victorious
life comes to a climax in the matter of soul-winning.
We know that soul-winning is the one matter dearest to the heart of God. "This is a faithful saying,
and worthy of all acceptation, that Christ Jesus
came into the world to save sinners" (1 Ti 1:15).
Jesus Himself said about Zacchaeus, "For the Son
of man is come to seek and to save that which was
lost" (Lk 19:10). We are told that in heaven the
one thing that causes rejoicing is the salvation of a
sinner. "I say unto you, that likewise joy shall be
in heaven over one sinner that repenteth, more than
over ninety and nine just persons, which need no
repentance" (Lk 15:7). If you want to do the thing
that is most important, then win souls. If you want
to be occupied with the thing that pleases God most,
then win souls.

First of all, soul-winning is such a worthy goal
that it makes all of life worth living, makes any in-
cidental pleasures of worldliness and sin seem worse
than useless if they hinder the blessed work of winning souls. To be absorbed in the greatest task in
the world and have all one's powers, all one's en-

ergy and enthusiasm harnessed in this great work certainly does simplify the matter of living right. Everything seems to fall into proper focus when one gets to doing the greatest business in the world. Many Christians, seeking the trifling pleasures of the world, are trapped by devices of Satan because they do not have an all-consuming passion that makes it worthwhile to live right, worthwhile to pray.

Some of us have worked on a farm and have driven big teams of four or six horses or mules. I assure you, many lessons can be learned from horses.

What a task it is to drive four horses to an empty wagon when they are hitched with two as a lead team, and two as wheel horses. If the driver does not watch, the lead team will slow down too much and the singletrees will hit their heels, or the tongue of the wagon will poke them in the rump and there will be a startled horse kicking in surprise and the whole team upset! Or, if the lead team goes too fast, they will pull the wagon up on the heels of the wheel team and they will bump their legs on the singletrees. Or, the wheel team will not follow the lead team exactly and so there may be a mix-up. But just put several tons of weight on the wagon and in a moment all the difficulties are gone. Each horse buckles down to his job and automatically stays in line. The wheel team cannot pull the wagon fast enough to run the tongue into the lead team. The lead team cannot pull the wagon up on the heels of the wheel team.

So it is that a great goal and a tremendous occupation with the most serious and blessed thing in the world can straighten out everything in the life of a Christian.

As a youngster I once worked a team of four horses and mules abreast to a big double-disk turning plow. Two of the team were wild young mules and as I drove into the field, before I got the plow into the ground, those two young mules got excited and bolted. They dragged the other team and the plow and me right along with them, and there we went, cavorting across the field! But I reached quickly for a lever and let the plows down deep. What a change! As the big disk-breaking plows caught hold, they began to throw the soil in great arching streams. The wild mules suddenly found they were doing all they could do, going zigzag across the field, pulling a plow that normally all four were needed to pull. That took the wind out of their sails mighty soon! Soon, sweating and panting, they were glad enough to stop. I drove back to the edge of the field, got my furrow running straight and had no more trouble with the young mules.

You see, many a young mule of a Christian gets off the track unless he gets some consuming passion for which it is worth giving up everything else. Soul-winning is the one greatest thing in the world.

What is there in all the universe that one could do which would have a reward for millions of years to come, like soul-winning?

I do not wonder that the Bible says, "He that winneth souls is wise" (Pr 11:30). He is not only wise for the next world, but wise for this world because it will save much heartbreak, it will still the siren voices that would mislead him and will give him strength to resist temptation. The soul-winner has the best chance in the world to live a life of victory.

The truth is that God cares so much for His soul-winners that He puts a protecting wall about them. In John 15:2 Jesus said, "Every branch in me that beareth not fruit he taketh away: and every branch that beareth fruit, he purgeth it, that it may bring forth more fruit." The Christian who does not win souls may be handicapped, he may be turned over to temptation. But every branch that bears fruit is purged by the loving hand of the Husbandman so that it may bring forth more fruit. Oh, how dear to God are the soul-winners who enter into the burden of Jesus for dying sinners!

When the Israelites were brought out of Egypt to go into the land of Canaan, God gave some very strict instructions. In the siege of any city, God said, "Only the trees which thou knowest that they be not trees for meat, thou shalt destroy and cut them down" (Deu 20:20). If they needed logs to make trenches or bulwarks against a city, they could cut down oak trees or the trees which did not bear fruit. But fruit trees had to be saved. By this God meant, surely, to give a spiritual lesson to Israel and to us. God loves His fruit trees! God will protect His fruit trees from the destroying hand that is turned against fruitless Christians.

The Christian who does not win souls lives in disobedience. He is not occupied with the main thing that concerns God. He is not obeying the Great Commission. He has already sinned in this matter and he will doubtless fall into many other sins. So, dear Christian, if you want to live a victorious life, get on the main track, get busy about the thing dearest to God's heart, start out to obey the one Great Commission, the marching orders for church, preacher, and individual Christian. Soul-winning work is a blessed, protected highway for God's choicest saints.

Now my task is done. I have found that a Christian may live a triumphant, happy life. A Christian can walk in the light as He is in the light, and the blood of Jesus Christ cleanses continually. What a blessed fellowship in this holy walk the Christian may have daily with God!

> Nothing between my soul and the Saviour,
>   Naught of this world's delusive dream;
> I have renounced all sinful pleasure,
>   Jesus is mine; let nothing between.

Nothing between like worldly pleasure;
  Habits of life, though harmless they seem,
Must not my heart from Him ever sever,—
  He is my all, let nothing between.

Nothing between, e'en many hard trials,
  Though the whole world against me convene;
Watching with prayer and much self-denial,
  I'll triumph at last, with nothing between.

Nothing between my soul and the Saviour,
  So that His blessed face may be seen;
Nothing preventing the least of His favor,
  Keep the way clear! Let nothing between.

                                C. A. TINDLEY

Moody Press, a ministry of the Moody Bible Institute, is
designed for education, evangelization and edification.
If we may assist you in knowing more about Christ and
the Christian life, please write us without obligation to:
Moody Press, c/o MLM, Chicago, Illinois 60610.